Archangels

Unlocking Secrets of Working with an Archangel, Spirit Guides, and Guardian Angels

Free Bonus from Silvia Hill available for limited time

Hi Spirituality Lovers!

My name is Silvia Hill, and first off, I want to THANK YOU for reading my book.

Now you have a chance to join my exclusive spirituality email list so you can get the ebooks below for free as well as the potential to get more spirituality ebooks for free! Simply click the link below to join.

P.S. Remember that it's 100% free to join the list.

~~$27~~ FREE BONUSES

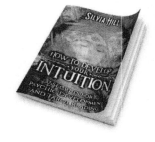

- 📖 9 Types of Spirit Guides and How to Connect to Them
- 📖 How to Develop Your Intuition: 7 Secrets for Psychic Development and Tarot Reading
- 📖 Tarot Reading Secrets for Love, Career, and General Messages

Access your free bonuses here
https://livetolearn.lpages.co/archangels-paperback/

Table of Contents

Introduction

Getting a basic understanding of what angels are is the key to a deeper, more meaningful spiritual life for anyone remotely interested in their existence. If you want to learn more about angels, then you'll enjoy this book. It is ideal for anyone who has a basic understanding of the Bible but is also an easy-to-read entry point for those who do not know much (or anything) about angels.

The Bible contains a substantial amount of information about angels, but there are many other books on the topic by authors who claim to have insider knowledge on angels. They claim to have access to the spirit realm, allowing them to reveal secrets people are not supposed to know. However, these secret insights are often nothing more than conjecture mixed with ancient superstitions. The information in this book is different as it is based on what scholars and historians agree can be verified as facts.

The truth is that angels exist, clearly and undeniably, and the strongest reason for believing that they exist in the first place is because of the miraculous stories that people have written and told about them, not to mention the substantial amount of evidence that skeptics cannot easily explain away. This book is meant to answer many questions you may have thought about – but never had the chance to explore fully.

This is not just a book but an opportunity to change your life by moving into a new way of thinking about angels. Armed with this book, you'll have the knowledge and credibility to openly discuss what you have learned about the archangels in your life. You can accurately explain who they are and why they are important in your life. Most importantly, you can be sure that your thoughts and beliefs are based on fact, not myth, not conjecture, but fact. If you are ready to move from being a curious onlooker of the subject of angels to a knowledgeable believer, then this book will be an invaluable resource in your journey. Let's get right into it.

Chapter One: Angels and Archangels 101

Angels are beings who exist in many cultures, religions, and beliefs. Some believe they are spirits of deceased people, while others believe they are simply symbols of grace. They are typically described as beautiful human-like beings with radiant skin and wings who descend to Earth to bestow their grace upon mortals. The word angel comes from the Latin word *angelus*, meaning "messenger." The oldest myths of angels date back to the Mesopotamian and East Asian cultures. These cultures created mythical beings to interpret the world and guide humans. These myths involved angels who carried prayers from Earth to heaven and the gods who relied on them for messages sent by humans to the heavens. The belief in angels became more widespread during the Jewish exile to Babylon when priests and scribes began interpreting the Mesopotamian stories and incorporating them into their religion.

Although the idea of a god on high came from Mesopotamian culture, Christians began to believe that God's heavenly hosts did not simply serve as messengers between humans and heaven. Instead, God created them as a way for humans to know that heaven existed. They were believed to appear in dreams and visions, considered holy messages by the people who had them. However, they were also believed to interact with humans once they began to fall out of favor with their Heavenly Father. Turning away from God would result in an angel becoming demonic and manipulative.

Islam offers an interpretation of angels that is very similar to Christian angelology. Angels are considered divine beings created by Allah who carry out His will on Earth. Muslim angels are also called angels, although Islam does not believe in heaven. They are believed to embody God's knowledge and power and have no physical bodies. However, their influence is not restricted to the afterlife. Many Muslims believe angels are found worldwide, acting as divine agents to those who deserve them.

Although angels are believed to carry out God's will and act on his behalf, Christianity views angels as having a more protective role. They are not merely messengers between humans and heaven but also serve to protect people from evil forces. In Christianity, they are often called guardian angels and are believed to be assigned to everyone at birth. Unlike Islam and Judaism, Christianity teaches that angels have a physical body, although they do not eat, drink, or experience any physical pleasure. Furthermore, the Christian belief is that angels are the only beings that God created before the creation of humans. They are considered to be immortal, divine, and timeless.

Judaism does not subscribe to the concept of guardian angels. However, it does believe in angels who watch over and protect people at all times. The Jewish laws that govern every aspect of a person's life require angels as messengers and intermediaries between man and God. Angels are believed to be bound by God's commandments and do not stray from them. They have no free will nor desire because they serve as extensions of God's will in relation to humans.

The Hindu religion considers angels as beings who exist in the natural world and provide guidance to humans. Angels in Hinduism are considered to be highly evolved spirits who have existed since the creation of the universe but never incarnated as physical beings. They are believed to possess multiple aspects that can be altered at any time. For example, if humans commit a sin like greed, then the angelic forms of greed will appear on Earth while those aspects of goodness remain unaffected.

Zoroastrianism believes in a good and evil god and in the existence of angels, although they are not believed to be divine beings. In fact, Zoroastrians believe that there are three separate groups of angels:

- Amesha Spentas, who govern goodness
- Yazatas, who govern the elements
- Daevas, who are described as evil spirits

Although each group represents one particular characteristic, Zoroastrians believe the world is made up of malevolent and benevolent forces. This world is represented by the struggle between these two forces, which are always in conflict. Zoroastrianism does not believe that angels have individual wings, nor do they carry out God's will. Interestingly enough, the Yazatas are thought to inhabit the bodies of humans who were once followers of Zarathustra, the prophet of Zoroastrianism. This taught that by becoming a follower of Zoroaster, followers would become divine themselves.

Buddhism does not support the concept of angels but does encourage belief in spirits. These spirits exist in two separate areas, the heavens and the Earth. Unlike angels, who are considered to be divine beings with no physical form, Buddhist spirits are embodied by humans who have died. A bodhisattva is believed to be a being whose soul has reincarnated into a celestial or earthly form so that it can achieve enlightenment and assist humans on Earth.

The Japanese religion of Shinto is based on a belief in angels. In fact, the Japanese belief holds that the practice of having a shrine at one's home has been passed down from ancient times and was first performed by an angel. The concept of angels in various religions has evolved over time and taken many forms of development, geography, and culture. However, there are some common elements found in each religion. Guardian angels protect their human charges, humans who will one day become angels themselves, physical bodies that allow them to interact with humans, and the interaction between good and evil forces on Earth.

The Angelic Hierarchy

The concept of heaven is a powerful one that has captured the interest and imagination of people for thousands of years. After all, who does not want to believe that the beings who are from such a phenomenal place can look out for us on Earth? However, it raises the question of whether all angels are equal in rank and power. The answer seems to be no. Why is this? The answer lies in the writings in the Bible, which speak of a hierarchy of angels between heaven and Earth.

In 1513 AD, a German monk named Fra Luca Gauricus published a book titled Dialogues on the Life of Jesus Christ. It was first printed in Latin and later reprinted in several European languages such as French, German, Italian, and Spanish. In this book, Gauricus included an allegorical painting depicting the story of how an angel tempted Adam and Eve to eat from the tree of knowledge of good and evil. There were two angels depicted in this work, one who tempted Eve and another who came to her rescue (or intervened).

These two angels, who represent a very different sort of angelic being from everything else we have mentioned so far, are considered to be one of Christianity's most important and unique angels. The detail in Fra Luca's painting depicts them as having six wings and no legs. They are described as being dressed all in white with flowing hair and a crown or as a tall man with a long robe. This depiction has stuck to this day and is used by some Christian churches in their artwork.

Some people may be aware of the angelic hierarchy but may not understand how it operates. The hierarchy has to do with the work of the angels. The most famous angel is Michael, but many others above and beneath him carry out different tasks. It is all part of their role as agents of God's will in the world, which is to help humans accomplish their purpose on Earth. This hierarchy is divided into nine ranks known as choirs, and each possesses distinct characteristics identified by their particular level in the hierarchy.

The Seraphim

The highest rank in the angelic hierarchy is that of the Seraphim. They are considered to be the closest angels to God and therefore receive his love and light. They are considered to be the guardians of the throne of God. Traditionally, they have six wings and two sets of eyes. The first set is in the front, where there are two eyes known as "the eyes of love," and the second set is on top, which can see everything at all times. Above their heads is a halo or ring like a rainbow that shines with light like a thousand suns combined into one great brilliance. The Seraphim are also said to have feet of gold and hands like crystals. In the Old Testament of the Bible, there is a reference to seraphim residing in the Temple of Solomon. They were said to be the angels who guarded the Ark of the Covenant and served God. There is evidence that people worldwide worshiped seraphim in ancient times, including in India, China, Japan, and many other places across Europe.

The Cherubim

The next highest rank after the Seraphim is that of the Cherubim. The Cherubim are described as having four faces and four wings. They are also said to have two arms and a breastplate embellished with precious stones. The cherubim appear to be the same as the seraphim but have just two pairs of wings and one pair of arms. The Cherubim are known as protectors who guard God's throne in heaven. They are also said to be the guardians of God's will on Earth. In fact, they are even mentioned in the Old Testament concerning Adam and Eve. When they left their Garden home, they were stationed outside Eden with a flaming sword to guard the path to the tree of life. The Cherubim are a symbol of innocence and purity, and because of this, many people like to put them in their artwork or religious homes so that they can connect with these qualities within themselves.

The Thrones

The next rank after the Cherubim is that of the Thrones. They are said to be a flaming wheel with a thousand eyes, and God sits in the center of this wheel. It is believed that this is the same wheel described in the book of Ezekiel. It states, "*Above it (the throne) were the wheels of fire, and all four wheels had the same likeness.*

The appearance of the wheels was like a wheel in the middle of a wheel". These wheels have eyes made of fire, and they are not just there to be decorative but to represent the presence of God and his will on Earth. They stay nearest to God and remain in his presence always.

The Dominions

This rank of angels are the keepers of divine order, think middle administration. They are in charge of the universe's rules, laws, and regulations and hence are concerned with ensuring that all humans follow these laws. They also oversee all human activity, which is why they can be considered a task force investigating social misconduct. This order of angels is also known as Hashmallim and is seen as responsible for earthquakes, storms, and other natural disasters. However, it is implied that they get these orders from God, who sends them to do his will. The leader of this group is the angel of mercy, Zadkiel.

The Virtues

With a form like orbs of light, these angels are charged with the maintenance of nature. Throughout history, the Virtues have been known as healers and can be thought of as responsible for ensuring that nature functions optimally. They bestow miracles upon those who deserve it, as instructed by the higher-ranking angels. In the Bible, it was said that these angels were present when Jesus ascended into heaven.

The Powers

The Powers are variously described as a floating mass or cloud of fire or possessing the form of a winged bull. They are the closest ranks to humanity and, thus, have certain charges related to human affairs. They look over justice in society by ensuring everyone understands what laws and rules apply to them. They are responsible for the welfare of humanity and are often charged with teaching. However, like humans, they are vulnerable to acts of sin and can become immoral.

The Principalities

This rank of angels is often depicted in art as light rays. They are thought to be in charge of the individual nations of the Earth and religious groups, but they also have a responsibility for all humanity. They are in charge of all situations involving law, science, and technology. They also govern the activities of the regular angels below them and ensure that everyone carries out their tasks properly.

Archangels and Angels

Archangels are the highest rank of angels. Their job is to help people and bring them closer to God by guiding them on their path through life and sometimes giving them messages from him. They have been known since the earliest times as presences who watch over specific affairs of man. The word archangel comes from the Greek *arkhangelos* meaning "the chief angel."

In practice, there are only four archangels: Michael, Gabriel, Raphael, and Uriel. However, Enoch's book mentions an extra three, Remiel, Saraquael, and Raguel. The name Michael is derived from a Hebrew word meaning, "He who is like God." The name Gabriel means "the strength of God," Raphael means "God's healing," and Uriel means "light of God" while also having a reference to being in the presence of God.

Pre-Christian views on archangels vary significantly from those held today. For example, in early Christian thought, the archangels Michael and Gabriel were thought to function as bringers of guidance and revelation, while Raphael was considered more of an aesthetic figure. Today, most modern theologians regard Michael as the leader of the other archangels and Gabriel as the sole angel who appeared to Mary in the New Testament.

Michael the Archangel, also known as the Ancient of Days, watches over all of humanity. He is the chief angel in charge of all matters concerning mankind. Although many Christians see him as ruling the angels, he does not do this directly. Rather, he is the leader of all archangels because he is said to be among the oldest angels in existence. In some legends, he appears to humanity members with unique qualities and needs and often grants special powers to those who need them most. Michael was said to be present when Jesus ascended into heaven and is often painted in Christian art as wearing scale mail armor that covers his legs and feet, with his armor being decorated by various small stars or crosses.

Gabriel the Archangel is seen as the messenger of God. He is said to be the one who brings messages to man from God and gives guidance to those who want it. In the New Testament book of Revelation, he is given a central role in bringing news of the story of Jesus Christ's return to earth and his final victory over Satan. When Jesus was taken up into heaven, it was Gabriel that brought this news down to Mary, his mother.

Raphael the Archangel is seen as a healing angel and will visit sick people in their dreams with messages from God if they require healing. He is often depicted as wearing red robes and having wings, signifying his role as healer and guide.

Uriel the Archangel is seen as the angel of wisdom and repentance. He is said to be the cherub tasked with guarding the gate of Eden. He is also the angel of death that swept across Egypt on the Passover and the angel sent to warn Noah about the flood.

Archangels have appeared in various religions across the world. In Islam, the Archangel Gabriel appeared to Muhammad and revealed the Qur'an to him. In Judaism, Gabriel is the angel of death. In Christianity, he appeared to Mary and informed her of the birth of Jesus. Gabriel is also believed to be the angel who will sound the trumpet on the last day, but this is a Christian belief because the Muslims believe it is the Archangel Raphael who will perform this action.

The term "archangel" is also used in the Zoroastrian tradition. Of the seven Holy Immortals, two are archangels, Mithra and Rashnu. Here, they serve as intermediaries between God and man. In Wicca, archangels are often called "guardians" or "elemental kings." They have been reinterpreted as identical to other authoritarian deities from other religions, such as Jehovah and Satan, although most adherents acknowledge them as separate beings.

Archangels have been depicted in many styles and types of clothing. In Christian art, Michael is often shown wearing a winged helmet and is often carrying a flaming sword. Gabriel is commonly seen as wearing a light-blue tunic and has wings, which is his usual appearance in the book of Revelation. Raphael was believed to wear the same clothing as Michael but with a red cape or robe. Uriel has been portrayed with armor like that of Michael but without the wings. However, Uriel can also be seen as having black robes and usually has a spear in his right hand, which references his role as an angel of death.

Archangels have been depicted in religious art for several centuries, with early examples of archangel art dating back to at least the 1st century. The oldest surviving representation of an angel is from the 10th-century "Book of Durrow." The painting depicts a winged figure with a halo sitting on top of a tree trunk, which symbolizes death. In some depictions, this image is accompanied by another figure with outstretched wings and a halo. This second being has been interpreted as an angelic demon who takes control of the first and represents death. Later Christian art views Michael as the most important archangel, and he often appears in paintings or sculptures holding his flaming sword. In this way, he can be compared to the Hindu god Shiva, who protects the world with a divine sword. An early depiction of Raphael is by the Italian Renaissance artist Giovanni Lanfranco who painted him with a scallop shell in his right hand. The scallop shell as a symbol is related to immortality since some believe that if – upon death – one has a scallop shell in their hand, they will become immortal.

In Occultism, Uriel has been viewed as a key spiritual force that can remove negative or evil spirits. Many modern-day occultists, however, believe that Uriel should be seen as the archangel who controls the forces of nature, while Gabriel controls the four elements, fire, earth, wind, and water. As well as this, they believe that Michael should be seen as being in charge of spiritual energies and all good things in life, while Raphael is in charge of healing and love. While this view may be popular among some occultists, it is not a view shared by many known mainstream religions.

The difference between Archangels and regular angels is an aspect of the archangel's role in the Judeo-Christian tradition. In the Bible, God sends regular angels to carry out his will, but the archangels are special angels who are given higher status and are more potent than other regular angels. The two most prominent archangels, Michael and Gabriel, were sent by God to carry out crucial tasks that affected all of humanity. Michael had a major role in defeating Satan and leading humanity to salvation, while Gabriel had a major role in revealing messages and prophecies from God to humans.

The Christian and modern-day Jewish beliefs in archangels are largely derived from their belief in angels and the angelic hierarchy. In Christian belief, angels have been seen as the messengers of God. Because of this, they are believed to have a hierarchical system of ranks. However, some Protestant churches do not agree with these hierarchies and do not believe that there is a hierarchy of angels. The Catholic Church believes that *there is* – but does not believe that these hierarchies are as strict or structured as they were in the past.

Frequently Asked Questions

Q: How many angels are there?

A: Scholars estimate anywhere from millions to billions of angels. Most, however, agree that there are at least several million.

Q: What does an angel look like?

A: There are many descriptions of angels and what they look like. In the Old Testament, they are described as winged creatures, and in the New Testament, they have human-like features and have been said to have wings and halos. Other descriptions say angels are tall with big muscles and radiant hair or skin. In other ancient texts, angels are described as being made entirely of light.

Q: Do Archangels have personalities?

A: Throughout most of the Bible, archangels are not given human-like personalities. However, in many modern religions, such as Judaism and Christianity, archangels are portrayed as being intelligent and having individuality.

Q: Do all religions have Archangels?

A: In fact, not all religions have archangels. Some religions, such as the Hindu religion and certain Native American religions, do not believe in archangels at all. Other religions, however, believe in archangels and call them different names.

Q: Do angels have a gender?

A: Angels are believed to be genderless. The genderless nature of angels is often debated. However, some religions believe that although angels have no gender, they still identify with a specific gender.

Q: Can I really connect to an angel or Archangel?

A: Connecting to an angel or Archangel is possible and has been done by people throughout history. A noteworthy example is the clairvoyant mystic Edgar Cayce, who was able to connect to Archangel Michael and receive detailed information about his role and the role of other angels.

There are many things to consider when thinking about angels and archangels. For example, every religion has its own interpretation of what an angel or Archangel is and how they should act or appear. Some religions believe that angels are winged creatures, while others believe that they are genderless beings. A few religions believe that angels are completely made of light and have no solid form. These opposing beliefs make it hard for people who practice different religions to agree on the identity of an angel or Archangel. However, many religions do not dismiss the role angels and Archangels play in the world. Almost all religions believe that angels have a significant role in life and can be used to help humans with their daily struggles and quests for knowledge. So, if you have ever wondered what an angel or Archangel is and their role, you may feel more comfortable knowing that in almost all religions, they are treated as pure beings whose sole purpose is to help humans.

Chapter Two: Spirit Guides Basics

Spirit guides are the unseen allies of your spiritual journey to help provide wisdom and insight. They exist to offer guidance and support through every step of life. Spiritual guides are not a religious idea but rather an ancient universal concept that can be found in many cultures across the globe. The guides may come in many forms, including animal familiars, angels, nature spirits, and even loved ones around you. They may be present in the physical world, the astral plane, or the dimension.

Guides can even be part of your higher self or a spirit form on another level entirely. They may appear and disappear, speak to us through our dreams, or come in a rush of energy and emotion. They can help us to heal emotionally, mentally, and physically. Sometimes they can even perform acts of magic for us as well. Though some can be messengers of healing, protection, love, and enlightenment, they are messengers of warning. Spirit guides serve as our guardians in the astral world, the plane we go to when we sleep or go into altered states of consciousness through meditation or shamanic work.

In ancient times, spirits were thought to inhabit every stone, tree, and body of water. Today, however, with science advancing rapidly, we are more aware that all things on the physical plane have a spiritual dimension. Ancient cultures believed that everything was made up of energy, not just the physical world but even our beings. The human body is made up of energy, and human beings themselves are also made up of energy.

Spirit guides are a part of this same energy, but on a higher level than we are. In other words, they are an integral part of our being that resides in many dimensions simultaneously, both in the physical plane and beyond. They are the fuel that keeps our spiritual journey running. Through them, we can gain access to a greater sense of self-awareness and information on how to deal with life's challenges. When we work with spirit guides, they can give us advice far more helpful than what we receive from friends or family members.

Throughout human history, people have felt that they were guided through life by unseen forces. They felt that their lives and destinies were planned out in advance and that there was a reason for everything that happened to them. This idea is expressed throughout many world religions, especially those from Asia and Europe, as well as Native American culture. It is a very comforting idea for many people because it explains things we do not understand about our existence here on Earth. Many of us yearn to have a deeper connection with our higher selves and the universe; spirit guides may be the missing link.

Spirit Guides in Native America

In Native American culture, the belief in spirit guides is very strong. When a child is born, a ceremony is performed in which the parents give the child a name for both their human and spiritual selves. Sometimes this is also done for an adult who may need to be reconnected with their spirit guides. A shaman, or medicine person, will be called to perform the ceremony.

Native American cultures believe that every individual has at least one primary spirit guide who is always there for us in our day-to-day lives. This can be an animal or other forms of nature, such as wind or water. These are usually quiet spirits who do not make themselves known unless someone is in danger or needs assistance. They are there to help us in our times of need but will always remain hidden from us unless we specifically call upon them. These are the spirits who guide us through major life events.

They will watch over us throughout our entire lives as we go through significant transitions and make big decisions. These guides work with other spirits to help provide guidance for each person's highest good. They are likely to appear at times of transition, helping guide people into a new direction or path. At other times, they may be seen during particularly difficult or upsetting moments, offering comfort and support to those who need it most.

Spirit Guides in the Bible

The Bible mentions spirit guides many times throughout ancient texts and scriptures. These passages tell of many spirits who watch over people throughout their lives, helping to guide and protect them. One of the spirit guides mentioned in the Bible is Gabriel, the archangel. In the book of Luke, he helps guide Mary through the birth of Jesus Christ. He assists her with protection and wisdom at a time when she has to make a very important decision about how to proceed with her pregnancy. Gabriel, who plays a central role in the story of Mary and Jesus, is an important spirit guide for many people because it is said that he comes to us through the Virgin Mary. The second time we hear of Gabriel is in the book of Daniel. He plays an important role in Daniel's life, protecting him from harm during the times of his greatest suffering and decision-making. This protection enabled him to fulfill his mission as God's chosen prophet. We learn that Gabriel has a special flair for ensuring those in need are protected and can do what they came here to do. This is why he is sometimes called the guardian.

The Book of Job tells us about another important spirit guide. Interestingly, this spirit guide is not one that anyone can see or hear as it is invisible and intangible, but we can feel its presence as it fills our days with comfort, peace, and protection. To say that this spirit guided Job would be an understatement because it is said that it protected him from all harm by traveling in whirlwinds at his side.

Spirit Guides and Shamanism

Much like Native Americans, shamanic cultures also believe in spirit guides and other spiritual beings who watch over each individual and help them throughout their lives. A shaman is someone who is called upon to help people through the use of spirit guides. They will meditate with them, pray to them, and commune with them in special ceremonies. These ceremonies are usually performed alone, but they can also be performed in groups under the watchful guidance of the shaman. During these special ceremonies, the shamanic practitioner seeks to contact their spirit guides with them. They do this through meditation and by making offerings and performing sacred dances. Shamanic practitioners believe that it takes a great deal of discipline to find your spirit guides and work with them personally. It also requires a great deal of trust in both the spiritual guides themselves and in the process of uncovering their true nature.

African Spirit Guides

African cultures believe strongly in the concept of spirit guides. Many African cultures have a spiritual leader who is known to have special connections to the spirits and knowledge of what is to come in the future. These spiritual leaders make their home with their people and are called their "spirit brothers." They tend to be very humble and respected and often do the exact opposite of what society expects them to do. They will spend most of their time in seclusion, out of sight, but are always with the people who they serve. They watch over these people and protect them from harm, sickness, or poverty.

In many African tribes, a person is born with a particular spirit guide who will remain with them throughout their lives. These guides help them see clearly and live a long, fulfilled life free of disease and other strife. In other traditions, the spiritual guide comes to people during times of transition in life. It may come at birth, death, or a major decision, such as an engagement or marriage. Some popular spirit guides in Africa are the Orishas, the gods and goddesses of the Yoruba religion. Despite originating in West Africa, these deities are also venerated in Brazil, Cuba,

Haiti, and other Caribbean countries. The Orishas are called upon to help people and answer their questions during difficult times, including death and loss. Well-known Orishas are:

- Sango (pronounced *"shahn-goh"* with an emphasis on the second syllable), the god of lightning and thunder
- Ogun, the god of war
- Osun, the goddess of love and femininity (pronounced *"Aw-shoon"* with an emphasis on the second syllable)
- Obatala, the creator
- Esu, the trickster (pronounced *"ay-shoo"*)

In the Rastafarian faith, the concept of a spirit guide is emphasized in their beliefs about Haile Selassie I. In the early 20th century, Haile Selassie was viewed as an incarnation of God who was sent to lead his people in Africa. Many Rastafarians believed that he would return physically to Earth after his death in 1975. Death is not considered an end but a beginning within this belief system. Therefore, they believe that Haile Selassie is still alive and has left his body to live among them on Earth as their spirit guide.

In Haiti, spirit guides can be found in almost all aspects of Haitian culture. It is believed that spirits play a large role in society and that everyone has at least one spirit guide accompanying them throughout life. Haitian spirit guide beliefs include everything from the ancestors that live in the forest to the spirits of plants and animals. In some parts of Haiti, religious leaders are believed to be spirit guides. These healers will use their powers to cure the ill or to bring prosperity or love into the lives of their people.

In African culture, spirit guides are believed to be able to communicate with the deceased and also hold power over the planet. They can be contacted through praying, dancing, or using sacred objects. African faith healers will often ask their gods and spirit guides for guidance when they perform a healing ceremony or divination. In these ceremonies, spiritual healers believe they can make contact with their spirit guides to gain insight or advice that they can use to help their patients.

Spirit Guides in Western Spiritualism

In Western Spiritualism and Occultism, spirit guides are very common. These spirit guides are believed to be invisible beings who can help people with their problems or advise them on what they should do in certain situations. Spirit guides can even allow people to reach out to them and talk with them by using an Ouija board or some kind of object which allows the guide to communicate on its own.

This concept of a spirit guide is similar to that of the shamanic practitioner but is not as commonly used in Western society because it is often viewed as a belief in magic or witchcraft. However, it is important to note that spirit guides are not exactly the same as spirit beings, such as ghosts or demons. Many cultures worldwide believe that spirits can be contacted through special rituals and ceremonies and are not necessarily evil or malevolent as they are perceived in Western mainstream religions.

Spirit Guides and the New Age Movement

The New Age Movement teaches that some gods and goddesses live on our planet and that they can teach us how to achieve spiritual enlightenment. To learn about these gods and goddesses and to ask them for advice or help, we must first recognize their presence in our lives and connect with them through meditation. Spirit guides can be contacted by many people, whether they are believers or not, in the New Age movement. This is because the practice of contacting spirit guides has become very popular today, especially among those who practice energy medicine. Some energy medicine practitioners believe that when you contact your spirit guides, you can use their power to heal yourself. By doing this, it is believed that you'll then be able to reach out to other people who may also need your healing power or advice.

Types of Spirit Guides

Spirit guides are often called upon to get advice or guidance on various matters or problems that someone may have. After all, these spirits can have great knowledge, wisdom, and understanding of the world around them. Your spirit guide is there for you to do just about anything you want them to do. They are there for you when you need to know what to do in certain situations, such as when you need help with a problem, advice on how to deal with certain people, or even when you need someone to cheer you on during difficult times in life. Your spirit guide does not judge you. They are there for you whether you are a good person or a bad person and whether you believe in a higher power or not.

Spirit guides can come into your life at any time. However, they will usually make their presence known when you need them the most, when you have a problem, or when something major happens in your life, such as moving to a new location or getting married. They can be people who have died and who still exist in our world as benevolent spirits; however, they can also be other entities like angels or animals. The following are some common spirit guides:

Spirit Animals: Many people believe spirit animals to be spirit guides, especially those who practice Paganism and Wicca. Many Pagans believe that each person has a sacred animal spirit that is familiar, who can help them perform spells and rituals. They say that you can create a bond with this animal through meditation when you are communicating with God or the Creator. The familiar is said to be able to protect its master from harm, especially if the two are paired together during rituals and spell casting. Within Native American society, the relationship between a magician and his familiar is like that of a dog and his master. A person's familiar will remain close to its master at all times, even when it has passed on into the afterlife. Types of animal familiars include snakes, cats, dogs, birds, etc. However, black cats are considered the most powerful animal familiars due to their ability to cause good and bad luck, depending on the situation.

Ancestors: In some cultures, the spirits of dead relatives are believed to be spirit guides. This is one of the most common types of spirit guides among African American spiritual healers and other cultural groups who practice religious ceremonies based on their dead ancestors. The spirits of the dead ancestors can be there to help you with your problems or to teach you how to live a better life. The spirits of your ancestors will also be able to teach you about their different personalities and how to learn from them and appreciate your unique life experiences.

Angels: Angels are believed to be the messengers of God and often work with other spirits to help people in need. They are known to be able to show you visions of the future, advise you on important matters, and help you with your problems. Whenever you feel like angels or spirit guides are around, there is usually a reason for it. Perhaps they are there to help you in your time of need, or maybe it is just part of their mission to watch over and protect you.

Ascended Masters: An ascended master is someone who has died and comes back to teach others about God or a higher power. These people have supposedly achieved higher spiritual enlightenment and are thus here to help you. They will be able to give you advice on how to live your life, achieve happiness, and avoid trouble in your life. The ascended masters are often the spirits of religious figures such as Jesus Christ, Buddha, Mary Magdalene, Confucius, and even the prophet Mohammed.

Elementals: Elementals are believed to be spirit guides and are also known as fairies, elves, or pixies. They are often associated with trees, water, and air and are sometimes thought of as nature spirits. They may appear in human form and can accompany specific humans throughout their lives. The elemental is believed to be able to create minor changes in nature that may include rain showers to help with drought conditions or make the sun shine brighter. They can also grant wishes, especially those involving love and luck.

Elementals are often associated with nature.

Higher Self: The higher self is also called the indwelling spirit, the true self, and is believed to be within one's mind or heart. It is said to have existed before birth and is within everyone. The higher-self guides a person through life, protects them, and helps them make decisions that are in their best interest. It also is said to be able to tell you what your purpose in life is and what your special talents are, and it may even give you the ability to see into your future.

People who have had Out-of-Body Experiences (OBEs) often report encountering spirit guides during their experience. Sometimes, these beings can give them advice or show them visions. Some people may also report contacting spirit guides while they are in a death-like state. During the time after death, a person may meet their spirit guides, who will provide guidance and assistance to help them through the transition period between death and the afterlife. At other times, spirit guides are said by those who claim to have OBEs to be manifestations of their higher mind. In this case, a person may make contact with their own Higher Self or their soul that has become separated from their physical body and is still wandering through the universe.

Why Should I Get in Contact with My Spirit Guide?

The term "spiritual" means something related to our consciousness or our soul. It can also refer to a divine entity or an unseen presence that we cannot explain with science and logic. In today's society, there is a great need to understand the importance of spirit guides in human life. Spirit guides can help you realize who you really are and your place in the universe. They can give you a glimpse of your true purpose in life and how you can easily fulfill it. If you let them, they will guide you through every aspect of your life, including your spiritual, emotional, and intellectual side. Spirit guides will always help you reach your full potential even if you think you know what is best for you. They will take you beyond the limits that were placed on you by genetics or bad experiences. When you understand and accept their role in your life, they will better guide you toward a greater understanding of God and the meaning behind all things.

Every person has a spirit guide. Learning how to communicate with this guide is important because you can ask them any question, and they will answer you. They will provide insight into your soul and help you find closure with past experiences. Spirit guides can help us in many ways, including manifesting our desires through their connection with the universe and helping us grasp the true meaning of our life experiences.

Real-life Accounts of Spirit Guides

Spirit guides have been witnessed and recorded in real-life experiences. Here are some brief examples:

- In 1975, a woman named Helen Smith claimed to have been in contact with her spirit guide, who she called Sophia, for 12 years. During this time, Sophia guided Helen through many issues that pertained to her life. She also helped to banish the spirits of those who were trying to do harm to her and her children in their home.

- Another woman named Sheila Wyatt claims that at the age of 14, she met a spirit guide who appeared in the form of a cat. This cat taught Sheila how to travel between parallel dimensions during astral projection and also how to heal using divine energies. Sheila uses this ability with her clients today by helping them heal illnesses through spiritual practices and energy work.

- A third-hand account existed in the book entitled "The World beyond Death: An Investigation of over 50 Near-Death and Other Experiences" by Dr. Raymond Moody. In this book, a man tells the story of how he was trapped in a well as a young boy. While trapped, he heard his spirit guide calling to him from above the well. The spirit said it was waiting for him to be rescued from the well and told him not to worry. The boy's father then found him and removed him from the well.

Although there is no scientific explanation for spirit guides, it is believed that we all have a spiritual element inside of us. We may never know why we are here, but there are things in life you already know about yourself that you did not pick up from your parents or other influences. Spirit guides can help us find these things about ourselves and teach us to be able to use them in our lives. They can also teach us about the universe and nature.

If you have never had an experience with your spirit guide, do not fret. Some people have never experienced the presence of their spirit guides either. Still, nearly everyone can experience its power and strength in their lives if they open themselves to its influence. The truth is, when you finally meet your guide, you will surely know it.

Chapter Three: Angelic Signs

Many people feel that angels are always there, giving us guidance and support. Whether we can see them or not, they always try to get through with messages for our benefit. What if you miss those signs because you did not know what they were trying to tell you? Understanding the signs is a great way to bridge the gap between angelic beings and humans. The most common signs include:

Noticing Their Presence

Do you ever feel as if someone is watching you when you are alone? While it is always nice to know that we are not completely alone in the world, this can sometimes be a little unsettling. This feeling is especially strong if someone seems to be following you around. According to ancient texts and lore, this is one of the most basic ways that angels tell us they are trying to send us messages. They will make their presence very noticeable if they want our attention until we get the memo. The contact can take any form, from soft tapping on your shoulder to a sudden chill in the air or even a sensation of someone walking up behind you. This physical contact can also be very subtle. Sometimes we can feel someone standing right behind us, almost touching our shoulders when we are, in fact, alone. The key is to look for these signs because they could be trying to get your attention.

Olfactory Sensations

When we think of angels, we think of them as very pure and divine beings. Since they are beyond time and space, there is no way of knowing that they are not constantly sending us smells that remind us of the purest things we have ever encountered. Whether it is the smell of flowers or a particular aroma that reminds you of your favorite childhood memory, this is a way that angels can get your attention. If you are having trouble understanding what your angels are trying to tell you, one of the best methods is to pay attention to what smells you are drawn to and the feelings they evoke in you. Olfactory sensations are a good indicator of what your angels are up to.

Meaningful Music

Angels can send messages through music.
https://pixabay.com/images/id-605422/

Have you ever heard music that inspired you so much that you started to feel like something better was coming? If you have been through a rough time and the lyrics touched your heart, or the melody just made everything seem right in the world, it could have been an angel singing to you. You may not think of angels having a voice at all, but they do have a way of expressing themselves through songs. It is also something we tend to give ourselves over to more easily than stimulation from the other senses, hence a very effective means of angelic communication. Some people claim they have heard celestial choirs while passing through state parks or even in their own backyard. Try listening to it next time as it is worth it if only to hear the sweetest sounds imaginable.

Messages in Dreams

Dreams are an effective way for angels to communicate. They can be very literal in nature or symbolic messages designed to tell us something that we need to know at that moment in time. Pay attention to what you experience in your dreams, and ask yourself if there is anything that needs to be addressed or made plain for you. The dream world is a very mystical realm, and our dreams can be a way for angels to talk to us. We should listen carefully because the messages are usually darkly poetic, but they are there if you know how to interpret them. These dreams also tend to be very intense, which is why we are so disoriented when we wake up. We are pulled back into our bodies, and the dream world starts to fade away. Sometimes the messages just come through in their entirety, but sometimes it is a matter of stringing together different things that are said to us over time.

Physical Symptoms

Your body constantly sends messages you may or may not pay attention to. Sicknesses, aches, and pains are signs that your body is giving off. These can be attributed to many things like stress, allergies, or our emotional state, but they could also be a way for angels to get our attention. The angelic realm sends vibrations through the atmosphere; sometimes, we pick up on those vibrations through physical pain. This is a sort of wake-up call that is designed to make us listen. The more we listen, the better we will understand. It is important to keep in mind that this should be taken into consideration with everything else. You do not want to assume every headache is an angel trying to make a point. You can best listen to your body and pay attention when it is giving off warning signals.

What Are Synchronicities?

Synchronicities are events or coincidences that seem to be meaningful. They appear to result from some cause beyond coincidence, such as intuitive causation. The word synchronicity was coined in the 1950s by psychologist Carl Jung. Jung noticed that people often experience coincidences related to their thoughts and feelings, and these events form a pattern leading to an insight or understanding. The events may seem random, but they often reflect a message that the person can use to understand something about himself or herself.

In many cases, this insight reveals some change in one's life direction or some opportunity. In such situations, the person feels they have gained an understanding of themselves or their life from this apparent chance meeting, encounter, or event. Synchronicity is the experience of meaningful coincidences resulting from divine guidance or spiritual meaning. Many types of synchronicities occur in almost everyone's life at some point. They can be triggered by a thought, feeling, or external events, and they can also occur randomly. Here are some common examples:

1. **A Meaningful Dream:** Dreams are internal events, allowing us to gain insight into our minds and feelings without outside interference. If a dream is particularly vivid and memorable, it may be trying to tell you something important. Dreams can also be prophetic or precognitive.

2. **A Coincidence That Seems to Be Triggered by One's Thoughts or Feelings:** Sometimes, you have a strong feeling that someone will call or visit, and they do. Things that are related to you in some way seem to turn up at the right time. You could be looking for something and find it right away, or have a need and immediately encounter the perfect solution when you least expect it.

3. **Fitting Circumstances:** Events that are related to the present situation are unusual enough to catch your attention and cause you to think, "That's strange." When something that seems out of place happens, we wonder why it occurred. If we remember dreaming about the event before it occurred, we may wonder if it has some meaning

or message.

Synchronicity is an experience reflecting a spiritual order underlying the universe. Some people believe synchronicities result from divine guidance or spiritual meaning. It is thought that these coincidences are not random but rather purposeful interactions of the spiritual world. These events should be distinguished from mere coincidence, which does not have any sense of meaningful connection attached to it.

Synchronistic events are related, even if there is no apparent explanation for why they occurred together. It just feels as though there is some kind of connection between them. There is a certain amount of feeling involved in synchronicity, and we can often tell when something is meaningful to us, even if we cannot explain why it happened. When synchronicity affects you, you may feel excited and stimulated, as though something important has happened. You may also notice a sudden shift in how you perceive the world around you.

Synchronicity is a phenomenon that could be seen as one of the subtle, energetic ways that angels communicate with us. They are trying to wake us up to specific messages about ourselves or our lives by guiding us toward certain information and situations. Think of how synchronicities can kick start our lives in the right direction, showing us what we need to learn, whom we need to meet, or where we need to go. We may know something intuitively, think it over, and put it out of mind only for something relevant, significant, or important to happen. For example, you may have been thinking about returning to college but dismissed the idea because you had more pressing matters to cope with at work. However, soon afterward, you are offered a promotion or have a friend or colleague mention that they are considering going to the same college. Or perhaps you received an interesting brochure in the post, and it turns out that they offer an evening class which you could fit in with your work. This would be an example of synchronicity where something happens that is related to your thoughts and feelings but unusual enough to make you think, "That's strange."

Angels are trying to get us to pay attention and notice what may be guiding us. They want us to notice that there may be more going on than we realize, so we can make the most of the opportunities which come our way. They are trying to wake us up to the fact that our life is not as mundane and routine as we assume but may contain much more than we know. They want us to take note of things that don't seem to make sense and ponder what may be happening behind the scenes.

Angel Numbers

Angel numbers are a series of repeating numbers – often appearing at a significant time in our lives. They are a form of synchronicity and can be considered personal messages from your angels or spirit guides. But why would your angels want to deliver messages to you using a series of numbers?

Your angels and spirit guides are non-physical beings who exist at higher vibrational frequencies than we do. At this frequency, they do not experience the limitations of time and space as we do, so they can see everything in the present moment. They know us better than we know ourselves and see the bigger picture in our lives. They can see the purpose behind what we experience and know what we need to learn. They can also see the future, and for this reason, angels use numbers in their communications with us.

Angel numbers are everywhere, even on lottery tickets and license plates. These special sequences of numbers often appear at a time when we are making significant decisions or changes in our lives. Like all synchronicities, angel numbers seem to reflect some kind of spiritual meaning or significance behind them. The angel number series is used as a way for your angels to remind us of what we are here to learn or help us along the path we need to follow. For example, if you have a series of repeating numbers like 1111 and 2222, then this could mean that you need to pay more attention to the thoughts and feelings you have at these times.

How do you know when an angel number is trying to communicate with you? One of the easiest ways is by looking out for repeating number sequences. This could be 11:11 on the digital clock in your car or home or 11:11 on license plates as you drive past them. Sometimes they just appear in random places as numbers, or they could be a sequence of letters or words, but the most telling sign is if you realize that you have been thinking of and seeing a series of numbers recently. You may have been having lucid dreams or repeating words and phrases in your head that are represented by the number sequence. This repetition can be associated with an event or personal decision that has improved your life. If these repeated thoughts and feelings are related to an important turning point in your life, then you can be sure that these numbers were sent to you by your angels.

The extra energy the angel number series provides can help guide you toward making decisions and choices most aligned with your greater good. The energetic pattern of the number sequence is like an energetic fingerprint, providing you with a sense of reassurance and direction when making challenging decisions. For this reason, it is considered a sign from your angels, who delight in showing us how they are with us every step of the way.

Angel Numbers and Their Meaning

Numbers are symbolic and have been used as a form of divine guidance since the time of the ancients. They were often used in religious rituals and worship to address spiritual beings or entities, especially in medieval times. It is believed that these numbers were intended to aid the gods or angels as a means of communication by providing them with a physical form. Numbers also have a powerful impact on the human psyche. We can use them to communicate on many levels with the universe, and they can be used for things like making decisions, setting goals, or even healing.

When you notice angel numbers in your life, it indicates that your angels want to communicate something to you. They want to help put things into perspective for you and reassure you that all is well. They also act like spiritual bookmarks, directing your attention to a special page in the book of your life that needs reading. They are indications that a new chapter is beginning or that you have reached a significant turning point. Here is a list of common angel numbers and their meanings:

- **111** is the most commonly seen number sequence from angels, appearing everywhere from license plates to digital clocks. These numbers indicate that new beginnings are on the horizon, supported by the universal forces of attraction and expansion. It signifies that you are moving in the right direction and that your desires manifest before your eyes.

- **222** is also considered a significant spiritual number, as it represents your angels supporting you through all aspects of your life. This number sequence can indicate that you have made an important decision or choice that is in harmony with a greater purpose, one which will bring prosperity and new beginnings into your life.

- **333** is the angelic frequency associated with universal love and the soul's ascension. These numbers may appear anywhere, from hotel room doors to store receipts. They are common in synchronicities when an important decision is being made, and they tell you that love and compassion are powerful forces in the universe.

- **444** is another number often seen in synchronicity, representing the frequency of truth and purpose. It is also associated with physical manifestation, so these numbers can signify that your desires are manifesting into form around you. When you see these numbers repeatedly, they indicate that your angels want to help you to tune into the purpose behind what you are experiencing or where you are heading in life.

- *555* is the number associated with change and transformation. Often this is associated with an upcoming event such as moving to a new home or starting a new job. It is also thought to be the number of change and transformation in personal relationships, so it could be a sign that you must put more effort into communicating with others around you.

- **666** is often associated with the devil or evil, but this association is not accurate at all. This number has nothing to do with evil; it simply means "fear not." According to numerology, 6 relates to man, and when you combine it with fearlessness (12), you get a "fear not" message repeated twice. The fearlessness relates to the universal Divine perspective and the number twelve's connotations of perfection, wholeness, and completeness.

- **777** is a universal sign of achievement and fulfillment, associated with growth and expansion in every area of your life. When you see these numbers, it means that you have overcome challenges in the past, and now you are moving forward into prosperity because of it. They may indicate that a great opportunity or reward is coming your way for all your hard work.

- **888** is the number of completeness. It signifies spiritual wholeness, divine connection, spiritual guidance, and freedom from constraints. When you see this number sequence, it indicates that you have attained conscious awareness and are receiving the guidance of your angels.

- **999** is a sign that your desires have been granted. It signals to all involved in your life that it is time to celebrate and often involves personal achievement or some form of recognition. These numbers indicate that you should take time to enjoy the moment because new opportunities will soon present themselves to you.

If you feel a little lost and confused, it may be the time to reach out to your angels. Whether or not you know it, they are there leading the way and trying to communicate with you. Look for the signs and if you cannot find any of them, ask yourself what is going on in your life right now that could use a little guidance. Then listen. Trust that they are there, even if they are not making themselves known.

Chapter Four: The Zodiac Angels

Zodiac symbols

While most of us are not zodiac sign-savvy, we have all heard of the concept. Zodiac is a term for the constellations of stars visible in the night sky. There are 12 zodiac signs, each of which has an archangel and several guardian angels who watch over those under them. The concept originates from astrology, which purports that cosmic correspondences exist between celestial bodies in our universe and people on Earth. These twelve constellations move backward through the night sky, completing one full circle in a year, and are visible in the Northern Hemisphere. The concept of the Zodiac is a very ancient one, dating back to ancient Babylon, but it has been used in different forms in almost every civilization. To understand your zodiac angel's true meanings and how it can affect your life, you need to be familiar with its primary qualities as an energy source. The stories behind each celestial being and its influence domain will tell you much about your character and potential. We will begin with a quick overview of the zodiac signs:

Aries: Aries is the first sign of the Zodiac, representing a life focused on action and adventure. The characteristic of Aries is a single-minded focus on what needs to be done, even in the face of opposition or danger. You are inclined to take risks, but an edge to your aggressiveness can land you in trouble. However, you are persistent and do not give up easily when achieving your goals. When you do succeed, though, it is probably because of your tenacity. Those born under this sign love to prove themselves, and they will succeed in many ways, but their dominating, domineering attitude gets in the way of their relationships, which may come off as selfish and demanding.

Taurus: You were full of potential and enthusiasm in your early years, maybe a little too much of both at times. You may have been unconventional and a bit subversive. You had incredible ideas but could not always follow through with them because you tended to get stuck in the planning stages. You have matured over time and learned to let things play out by themselves rather than planning them every step of the way. Your life energy has undergone a similar transformation, finally finding its own path rather than trying to control everything all at once.

Gemini: Your life has always been very complex, and you have always had to think on your feet, adapt to new situations, and improvise. You thrive on challenge and love change, new experiences, and being in the middle of things, at least when they are positive. When it comes to negative stuff, you tend to avoid it. You have a gift for conversation that others find refreshing. You never lie or evade the point. You always say what is on your mind, but this can come out in blunt statements, which can be hurtful.

Sometimes you talk so much that people get annoyed with you, but nobody can ever doubt your dedication and talent for communication.

Cancer: You have always been sensitive, perhaps too much so. You may have painful triggers in your life, especially if you suffered from abuse when you were a child. Even now, you take on people's pain as if it is your own. You need to learn to let go and learn how to protect yourself from situations that can be perceived as a threat but really are not. You need to learn to trust yourself and what you know about the world around you. In some cases, this may involve reevaluating your beliefs. Over time, you have learned to take care of yourself rather than relying on the moods and demands of others. You are intuitive and have a way of knowing what is right for you and what is not. You always follow a feeling in your gut.

Leo: Your life has always been about the big picture, but in many ways, it has been about pride more than anything else. You have high standards and a sense of moral obligation regarding justice and integrity. However, you must be careful that this does not come across as bossy or rigid because others can take it that way. You have to let things flow the way they are meant to rather than forcing them into a preconceived idea of how they should be. You must learn to trust others and let them grow at their own pace.

Virgo: This signifies service, hard work, health, and healing. You are so focused on the details and practicalities that you may miss out on bigger issues. It is important to look at the big picture in your life and be flexible when it comes to dealing with others. You like things neat, tidy, and well-organized, and, as a result, you may feel overextended sometimes. You may not have time to talk about things that matter to you, but you always have time to do specific and necessary things. You are an expert on details and practical things, which gives you a strong value system. However, it can be difficult for you to revel in your accomplishments, so sometimes it helps to take a step back from the day-to-day and just breathe.

Libra: Your life energy is balanced and harmonious but also flexible and creative. You are sensitive to your feelings and intuitive about people's intentions. The ideal Libra partner is someone who can be totally supportive and will not try to rush into commitment or force through change. You need a partner who is willing to work on the relationship, who will give you a lot of space and let you live your own life. You also tend to be practical and down-to-earth regarding others' opinions or values since your goal is always peace, harmony, and balance. This can lead you to compromise too much.

Scorpio: This sign is associated with passion, depth of emotion, and hidden desires. You can be combative at times and have great power potential. Sometimes this power is channeled into anger or frustration. Other times, it can move people into action for the greater good. You have been hurt before and know how it feels to be on the receiving end of pain. You are usually very aware of others' feelings, and you tend to put yourself in their shoes, putting your own needs on the back burner. You also have a sharp mind, with a laser-like focus on detail and nuances that other people are not so good at picking up on.

Sagittarius: Your life has always been one of adventure and excitement. You love the outdoors and are a bit impulsive. You like going off the beaten path, even when it means taking risks, not necessarily dangerous ones, but more choices or options that help you keep things exciting in your life. You like to expand your mind, keep up with the latest trends and ideas, and try new things. You are a risk-taker, but in a good way. You have never been afraid to do what seems right or just.

Capricorn: This is a sign associated with ambition and pride, the need to achieve, sometimes at the expense of others. You want the best for yourself and for those you love. You thrive when you have a challenge with plenty of material resources. You like stability and control but also enjoy getting together with large groups of people, but only if it is important to you. However, this may come across as selfishness or self-centeredness and can cause conflict in some situations. You like structure and order in your life, and you can be very persistent. You also tend to be on the conservative side when it comes to relationships. You believe it should always be planned and romantic, making you appear cold or snobbish.

Aquarius: Your life has always been about change, adventure, mystery, and connections with the world around you. You are a free spirit who loves traveling, exploring, and meeting new people from different backgrounds. However, this could also make you vulnerable to getting caught up in bad situations or people who are not good for you. You have a harder time committing to people and letting them entirely into your life, especially if you feel as if they are not living up to your expectations. At times, you can be inappropriate with people's emotions and may have trouble taking things seriously. You need to learn that for a relationship to be successful, it needs to be built on real love and commitment.

Pisces: This is a very sensitive and creative sign, which can lead you to be moody, hesitant, unpredictable, and not always sure of what you want. You like to feel connected to spiritual and cosmic forces and are often drawn toward the arts. You think deeply about life, death, love, and the details of your own personal relationships. Your creativity can lead you to have difficulty following through on plans that you have made, and this can frustrate you. When it comes right down to it, it's all about feeling emotions and connecting with others through those emotions. You can be intense and reserved, so you must learn to connect with others through communication and honesty. Speak your mind, be true to yourself, and let others do the same.

Corresponding Zodiac Angels

Malahidael of the Aries Zodiac

Malahidael means "One of courage" and is the sign's ruler, Aries. He symbolizes all energy and power and is a great inspiration for action and adventure. He is the angel of life and transmutation and is known to be strong yet gentle and kind toward others. Malahidael is portrayed as a warrior angel, and his color is gold or orange. He is closely accompanied by Ariel, the Angel of Instinct, a lesser-known guardian of the Aries Zodiac.

Asmodel of the Taurus Zodiac

Asmodel is the angel of Taurus and aids in teaching self-worth, courage, and balance. He is known to be a wise and powerful mentor who inspires us to reach higher levels of consciousness. His colors are red or orange, symbolizing strength, perseverance, longevity, and vitality. Asmodel supports the preservation of Nature through the wisdom that comes from spiritual teachings. He stays connected with the Earth Mother and is closely accompanied by Chamuel, the Angel of Compassion. Together, they provide the strength and courage needed to fulfill the quests of the Taurus, who may sometimes have difficulty finding their way in this world.

Ambriel of the Gemini Zodiac

Ambriel is the angel of Gemini and aids in teaching communication, action, and relationships. He also teaches spiritual lessons to assist us in developing our own inner wisdom. His color is silver or gray, and his energy can be described as cold yet emotional, mysterious, and charming. Mental clarity, awareness, and a dose of laughter and joy are vital to his teachings. He is accompanied by Kadiel, the Angel of Expression, who works closely with him to provide guidance and protection to those seeking it. Their energy combines to promote enthusiasm, creative thoughts, inspiration, and understanding to the Gemini.

Muriel of the Cancer Zodiac

Muriel is the angel of Cancer and aids in teaching courage, intuition, and awareness. She is known to be courageous, protective, and passionate in her teachings. Her color is green or blue and symbolizes a high level of wisdom. She teaches life lessons that give us the tools necessary to overcome our fears and create a feeling of safety and serenity. Muriel is also known as the angel of unconditional love and an energy healer. She uses her energy to balance the Cancer's emotional and intuitive feelings and manifest positive outcomes in all areas of their life.

Verchiel of the Leo Zodiac

Verchiel teaches us the importance of service, unity, and communication. He is also known to be brilliant, quick-witted, and intelligent, if a little eccentric at times. His energy can be described as playful yet powerful. His color is silver or red and symbolizes the element of fire. Verchiel teaches the power of faith, intuition, and self-worth to those who invoke him through prayer. He is closely accompanied by Raziel, the Angel of Mysteries and Secrets, who aids in revealing spiritual growth to those who ask for his assistance. Together, they work to bring about the highest level of awareness, manifestation, and power for all Leos.

Hamaliel of the Virgo Zodiac

Hamaliel teaches patience, health, and understanding. He is also known as the holy angel of flowers, herbs, and peace. His color is green or silver, and he can be described as introspective and wise. He teaches us to live in the present rather than dwelling on the past or worrying about the future. He is closely accompanied by Anael, the angel of truth and knowledge, who aids in illuminating the inner-self with understanding. The combination of their energies helps the Virgo Zodiac to reach the highest spiritual level of development, self-worth, and understanding.

Zuriel of the Libra Zodiac

Zuriel teaches us to live in service to others. He is also known as the holy angel of balance, truth, and knowledge. He is seen as a teacher of understanding, equality, and justice. Light blue or white (the colors of his wings) represents wisdom and truth. He teaches lessons that help us to heal through giving, as well as helping us to regain our natural state of happiness by communicating with others. Zuriel also teaches the concept of intuition by imparting lessons that open up our minds and hearts to seeing beyond what we know. He symbolizes both emotion and intellect, qualities accurately embodied by the Libra.

Barchiel of the Scorpio Zodiac

Barchiel is the angel of Scorpio and teaches lessons against lust, possession, and jealousy. He takes an intense interest in war, power, and all things of the mind. However, he also teaches that we must develop an acceptance of our own capacity for pain or suffering. His color, black or dark red, symbolizes power and knowledge. He lives in dark or intense energy and can be very persuasive in his teachings. For the Scorpio, he brings the light to illuminate the darkest corners of their mind. He teaches awareness of what is real and what is not. He is closely accompanied by Asmodel, who is the angel of Taurus, which represents the element of earth and helps to balance Barchiel's energy of power.

Adnachiel of the Sagittarius Zodiac

Adnachiel teaches us about the importance of love, happiness, and optimism. He is also known as the angel of power and independence. His energy is described as joyful, playful, and always seeking fun. He teaches us to connect with others deeper, helping them find their inner power and divine nature. He can also teach us about the patience, faith, and determination that are needed to rebuild our lives after a painful experience. His energy is golden or orange and represents solar energy and the element of fire. Adnachiel is closely accompanied by Zadkiel, who teaches about action, initiation, and freedom. Together, they can teach the Sagittarius about letting go of the past and healing from emotional trauma.

Hanael of the Capricorn Zodiac

Hanael teaches us the importance of love, hope, and wisdom. He is also known as a holy angel of acceptance and surrender. His energy is seen as intense, serious, and wise. He teaches us to surrender our fears and desires, change what we can accept and what we cannot, and have faith in life's lessons. Hanael guides us to apply our own unique gifts to help others in times of need, rather than allowing our personal needs to get in the way. His colors are royal blue or purple. Those who invoke him are said to be blessed with divine help that leads them to inner peace, prosperity, and happiness. He teaches the Capricorn to forgive themselves rather than judge.

Kambriel of the Aquarius Zodiac

Kambriel teaches us to live in a state of freedom and reject all things symbolic of limitations. He is known as the angel who can help us find our true purpose in life. He also teaches about patience, adaptability, healing, and the reality beyond what we can see with our earthly eyes. His energy is seen as pale blue. Together with his partner, Uriel, he can show the Aquarius that their past is not a burden to carry but rather an important part of their journey to enlightenment. He also teaches them to live in the moment rather than dwelling in worry about the future.

Amnitziel of the Pisces Zodiac

Amnitziel teaches us about responsibilities and commitment to others. He is also known as the angel of romance, passion, and psychic abilities. His energy symbolizes positivity, inspiration, and balance. Those who invoke him experience happiness and live in the present moment. Amnitziel imbues wisdom, strength, compassion, and integrity into his teachings. His color is blue or purple, representing the universe, angels, and higher consciousness. He is closely accompanied by Zaziel, the angel of guidance and knowledge. Together, they teach the Pisces that their dreams can come true and that love is more than just a feeling.

Chapter Five: Communicating with Your Guardian Angel

What are guardian angels? Are they spirit beings or physical entities? Do they have a set job description or responsibility? What can you do to attract one into your life? These are all questions everyone has wondered at some point in their lives. The guardian angel concept was first brought to public attention in the 1800s by a French poet named Ernest Psichari. Since then, interest in guardian angels has grown and sparked debate worldwide on what they are, what they do, and how people can connect with them.

To understand guardian angels, you must first look at the contrast between religions or belief systems that believe in them and those that do not. Some religions do not believe in guardian angels at all, while others use this concept as one of their central tenets. In either case, the different perspectives on guardian angels are intriguing.

The guardian angel is viewed as a spiritual entity that upholds the divine order of things by caring for those entrusted to it. The guardian angel takes care of people while they are alive and, depending on the belief system, after death. Some guardian angels are also viewed as a special set of helpers who have been chosen and assigned to care for people whenever they are needed. In this case, the chosen angel is treated as a personal guardian who, when called upon, does not simply do what is asked of them but also takes care of the person regardless.

Guardian angels are believed to have been created by God before the creation of humans, and it is believed that there is at least one guardian angel for each person. It is also believed that each guardian angel has different roles. For instance, some of them are assigned as healers, others are protectors, and some serve as messengers between humans and God.

Although guardian angels have been used by many religions to explain away unexplainable phenomena or to answer a prayer request, only Christians significantly believe in guardian angels. For Christians, the archangel Gabriel is known to be a protector and guide, while Michael is known as a defender against evil forces and an advocate against temptation. The guardian angel is said to be the Holy Spirit or God's emissary working right beside the person who was assigned them. The angel is said to not only help during times of need but also to send messages from God, fulfill prayers, and show itself to people in times of trouble. However, for Christians, guardian angels are also assigned at the time of birth and can change as the person's role in life changes.

The guardian angel concept is referenced in various religious texts. For instance, it is found in the Bible and in ancient Greek, Hindu, Persian, and Assyrian texts. These texts speak of angels who work to guide human beings in their lives and who, when they need assistance, do so in a very passive fashion. In other words, the guardian spirit is only there to help out if someone needs their help. They are never intrusive and do not step in unless it is necessary.

According to Hindu texts, guardian angels are associated with the gods and viewed as manifestations of godly powers. They are believed to be personified forces of nature and elements that keep all things in order, and they perform their duties in harmony with the laws of nature. They are said to be given orders by the gods, but they are believed to have free will and decide how to carry out their commands.

As mentioned earlier, not all religions believe in the concept of guardian angels. This applies to non-theistic religions, such as Wicca, Pantheism, and those who believe in reincarnations.

Instead, they are believers in spirit guides, a concept that is closely related to guardian angels. As with guardian angels, spirit guides are designed to be there for humanity and also do their best to help people succeed on their journey to greater spiritual understanding or enlightenment.

Guardian Angels in Esotericism

In esoteric circles, a guardian angel is any nonphysical entity protecting a person from harm or negative thoughts or emotions. What makes this form of a guardian angel unique is its ability to bring positive thoughts and ideas into your life by changing your perception of things around you. For example, a guardian angel can be used to change your thoughts about an argument with someone or your fears of a certain situation. They also come in handy when something bad happens to you, such as when you are in danger or need healing. In these situations, it is believed that the guardian angel intercedes and draws out the best version of you so that you do not have to fear what is happening to you. In such cases, the nonphysical being is responsible for the circumstances in which these things happen so that they are beneficial to the human involved.

There are different levels of guardian angels according to esoteric belief systems. For instance, in some understandings, the more evolved guardian angels that have already been sent to Earth only watch over you, and you can call on them for help at any time. In other belief systems, this is the first level of a guardian angel's existence, and when these spirits are considered to be older and wiser, they may listen to your thoughts and feelings and use it as a guide when helping you through life. As they grow in their expertise with you, they can make more proactive choices based on what you need at that time. You can also use these spirits to get advice on decisions that you need to make and how you can find the best alternative options for those decisions. Some esoteric groups also believe that everyone is assigned a guardian angel from birth. Here, it is considered the guardian angel's responsibility to guide their "protégé" throughout his or her life to achieve their full potential. It is believed that these entities are assigned to each person due to their life goals and reason for incarnation in this world. The guidance can come in various forms, from dreams to thoughts or even different intuitive feelings that may seem unusual at first but can all help you understand things about yourself and the world around you.

Getting in Touch with Your Guardian Angel

To begin a relationship with a guardian angel, it is suggested that one should begin with the more basic techniques of meditation. This can be done daily in the morning or evening. Once you meditate, getting in touch with your guardian angel or spirit guide may be easier. There are different ways to approach this relationship. It can start as a simple friendship or partnership that involves talking to the nonphysical entity and then moving into a more active phase in which the entity willingly helps you out on some level.

With guardian angels, it is believed that they have already chosen you and are already looking over you. However, they may need your help understanding what they can do to help you. If this is true, all that needs to be done is to open your mind and be receptive to such assistance. Meditating will also allow you to achieve an altered state of consciousness that will allow your guardian angel to communicate with you in a way that works for both of you. This is often simply a conversation between the two of you where one or both parties want certain things from one another. The key, however, is to believe that you will be heard and understood.

Suppose you require healing or assistance with a certain situation. In that case, you can ask your guardian angel for help, although it may take longer to get a response from them. This type of communication is more one-sided in that it involves someone asking for assistance or help with something, and then the being will respond as needed. It can be as simple as just a feeling that something has changed in your life since you prayed for help.

It is also believed that our guardian angels are always around us and constantly use their energy to protect us from harm. Here, it is considered to be important for us to trust our angels and let them know that we are aware of their presence and appreciate their help. If you are having a bad day or have recently been in an accident, you can ask a guardian angel for help at that moment. A way to open up communication is by saying the words "I need your help" or "I want your help." This will then allow the entity to work on helping you, which may be through sending some message through intuition or just through helping you to feel better.

The Power of Meditation

Meditation makes it easier to connect with your guardian angels.
https://unsplash.com/photos/rOn57CBgyMo?utm_source=unsplash&utm_medium=refe rral&utm_content=creditShareLink

Meditation is a technique that involves clearing your mind of thoughts and allowing intuition to come to the fore. If you are not familiar with this technique, it is simply the act of sitting quietly and focusing on nothing but your breath until you notice something new coming into your awareness. At this point, do not attempt to control or direct what thoughts come into your consciousness. Instead, simply watch them float by like clouds in the sky. It is believed that you can use this technique to develop a communication channel with anyone, including your guardian angel. This is simply a method of relaxation and meditation that will allow you to feel one with the universe in a very literal sense. Here, no words or thoughts need to be exchanged between two parties when using this method of communication. Instead, "feelings" will flow to and from your consciousness, allowing you to understand what the other being is trying to convey.

It is believed that when you are in a state of meditation, you are more receptive to messages from your guardian angel. Therefore, your guardian angel can communicate with you through meditation and other intuitive techniques. It is also believed that during meditation, it is possible for things of a spiritual nature to be sensed, although these spirits are not always voices or thoughts that can be easily understood. However, a common experience that one may have while meditating is when the body, mind, or soul feels lighter or different for the duration of the practice. You can also include guided meditation in your practice. This is where you go through a series of instructions from a recording or from another person. It allows you to relax your mind and focus on breathing, which will disconnect your conscious thoughts from the inner self.

How to Meditate

If you are interested in meditating, it can be as simple as taking the following easy steps:

1. Find a quiet place where there is likely to be no interruption.

2. Change into comfortable clothing and shoes.

3. Light a candle to put you in the mood for meditation. You can also use music or surround yourself with soft colors and gentle scents like lavender, sage, or rose petals.

4. Sit with your palms facing upward in your lap.

5. Close your eyes and breathe deeply into your diaphragm area. Diaphragmatic breathing will allow you to focus on the moment rather than on any other thoughts floating. Your breathing should be slow and controlled. Inhale through the nose while counting to two, hold this breath for two more seconds, and then exhale slowly out the mouth.

6. Continue breathing this way until you are comfortable with the process.

7. Do not struggle with any thoughts or images that may be floating around. If they come into your consciousness, simply let them pass by and continue with your breathing.

8. Once you are comfortable, invite your guardian angel to the room.

9. Ask for any messages or guidance from your angel.

10. See what images or thoughts come into your consciousness. This may take time, and there is no rush to make things happen.

11. When you have finished, imagine the light that comes from your guardian angel spreading over you until it fades away and leaves you feeling centered and relaxed.

You must keep the link between your conscious and subconscious minds open. This is known as the "flow of thought," and it allows your conscious mind to send messages and thoughts through to your subconscious mind. If too much information is coming from one channel and not enough from the other, it may result in confusion or even anxiety. However, when things flow smoothly between both channels, it will allow you to get in touch with your intuition and inner core self in a very literal way.

Other Ways to Contact Your Guardian Angel

Meditation is a great way to communicate with your guardian angel, but it is not the only technique out there. There are other ways that you can send messages to your guardian angel, and here are a few:

1. **Prayer:** Praying to your guardian angel can be extremely beneficial, and it is considered helpful to make a specific request rather than simply asking for help or guidance without giving any information. Here, you can put your request into words or write a prayer that includes what you want and thanksgiving for any help that has already been received.

2. **Writing:** When you need your guardian angel's help, you can write down your thoughts and concerns. Once you have completed writing, put the piece of paper away in a safe spot. This way, it does not require any action on your part to maintain your thoughts without forgetting them. You can also write down what it is that you need help with or ask for guidance or insight surrounding the issue at hand. In the following days, look out for any messages or signs that seem unusual or outside the norm. These can be from your guardian angel or other helpful entities.

3. **Visualization:** Visualization is the act of picturing something that you want to happen or something you need. Here, you can visualize what you want to happen and project this intention out into the universe. Once you have a clear picture of what it is that you need, it is believed that this picture will trigger your guardian angel to come to your aid. The picture will then appear in dreams and other forms of communication from your guardian angel.

4. **Pilgrimage:** A pilgrimage is more difficult to undertake than the other techniques, but it is believed that by walking along a path that has special significance for you, you can communicate with your guardian angel. This can also be done by going on walks in places that are significant to you or your spiritual experience. As with the other methods, you do not try to direct or control your thoughts. You simply let them go where they may find the answers that you seek.

5. **Telepathy:** Your spoken communication with a guardian angel may take the form of "telepathic" communication. This is where it differs from other alternative forms of communication that are common and accepted within mainstream belief systems. Here, actual words are exchanged between the two parties, but nobody can hear those words or understand what is being said. It can be as simple as one party just sending off messages and images to the other without anybody else knowing about it or being involved in the communication process.

Maintaining the Angelic Connection

Once you have interacted with your guardian angel, you should be open to a continued relationship with them. In this way, even if you are not actively thinking about them or their existence, being in contact with your guardian angel can still benefit your life. Here is how you might maintain a connection:

- **Relish the Good Feelings:** You can positively reinforce the positive feelings that come from connecting with your guardian angel. When you find yourself experiencing these good feelings, gratitude for these emotions should flow readily into your life.

- **Be Aware of the Signs:** If you have contacted your guardian angel and have been receiving help, it is important to know the signs they may send your way. While it may take a while to get used to trusting that your guardian angel is helping you, it is important to begin looking for signs of their existence. If you can begin recognizing these signs, you can also begin rewarding yourself with kind thoughts and gentle words.

- **Record the Experiences:** If you are having a lot of interaction with your guardian angel, it can be helpful to make notes about what you are experiencing. This will help you better understand how helpful your guardian angel is, how often you communicate with them, and the types of things they help you with. It will also allow you to better recognize signs from them and understand their existence in your life.

The Importance of Gratitude

It is very important to show gratitude to the guardian angel that has been helping you along your journey. Even though you have endured negative or unfortunate circumstances, it is very important to remember that you were guided into these situations. Turn your disappointments into lessons and celebrate the moments when things work out for the best. Showing gratitude for all that happens to you allows your guardian angel to feel appreciated and continue to help you when you need it. One way to show gratitude is by acknowledging your guardian angel's presence and thanking them for their role in your life.

You can also show your gratitude by blessing others who are going through difficult circumstances. If someone is having a hard time, you can offer them words of encouragement and show them that you support them. You can even bless others by praying for them or sending them positive energy. You can also show gratitude by giving thanks for the gifts that you have in your life. This could be the gift of family and friends, health and shelter, food, water, and everything else you have and feel grateful for.

Chapter Six: Connecting with Angelic Beings

In chapter five, we talked about guardian angels, what they are, and what they do for us. In this chapter, we will explore ways to contact any angelic being. Please note that not all beings have the same capabilities, and messages can be conveyed in several ways. These beings are generally found in the angelic realm, an expansive place, so preparing before you venture out there is not a bad idea. When working with an angel, it is important to understand that they can appear however it is most comfortable for them.

It may help to have a question or request in mind when you go out looking for angels. It is also important to remember that not all beings can interact with humans, and among those that can, not all of them will. You must also be open to the possibility of seeing things or undergoing experiences that may not make sense or seem logical. Angels can be quite playful, so it is a good idea to keep an open mind and know that you are on a journey of discovery.

To begin your search, pick a spot where you feel comfortable and familiar. Remember that all information is energy, so to get the best results, work in a space that is clean and clear of clutter. The area should also have good lighting and be well ventilated. I recommend that when you are speaking with an angel, you should be sitting comfortably and relaxed. Having a journal and pen next to you for notes is helpful. You'll also want to ensure that you are physically comfortable, so wear something loose-fitting and soft like cotton.

It is best to start with a prayer or meditation to help center your energy. Being centered will help you remain open and focused. Once you enter this space, it is important to remember that there are no mistakes here; it does not matter if you do not "feel" anything the first time out. Remember, this is a process of discovery not just for yourself but for the angelic beings.

The Importance of Spiritual Protection

Before you begin your search, it is important to consider your spiritual protection. We all come into this world with a predetermined level of protection, depending on our karma. The three basic layers of protection are:

- Our physical bodies
- The energy field (or aura) around our bodies
- The chakras or energy centers in our bodies

The physical body normally provides the first layer of protection from birth until death. However, we can influence this by poor lifestyle choices such as eating poorly, not hydrating enough, not getting enough rest, and so on. This is why we need to take the best care of ourselves physically, to remain in the best health possible. The second layer of protection comes from our auras, which help to keep out any negative energy. If the aura is cleared in or around the body, then it is easier for us to cleanse and heal since there is nothing to block our energy. One of the best ways to clear auras is through Reiki, which can be done quickly and easily. Another thing to remember about auras is that they change daily, and it takes time for them to recover.

The third layer of protection comes from the chakras, which are like psychic batteries that help keep our energy flowing freely. When we have blocked energy, the chakras are like useless batteries. To use them again, they need to be charged. This is best done through meditation and other forms of energy work. When clearing auras, it is best to clear each chakra in turn, starting with the base (root) chakra at the bottom of the spine. This will help to reset blocked energy and give you a boost of energy. During clearing sessions, it is also important to remember to let go and be gentle, as even the best intentions can cause harm if done improperly.

Before venturing into the spiritual realm in search of angels or for any reason at all, your protection should be priority number one. This is especially true when you are seeking to connect with angelic beings. The reason for this is simple, angels can see a person's entire aura, and they can read your life story like a book. The more they can see, the more they will know about you. This can be either good or bad depending on whom you are speaking with and whether they like what they see. You'll also be vulnerable to any negativity that wants to penetrate your auric field.

Many techniques can be used to provide a shield of protection, and these techniques have been around for thousands of years. Different techniques work for different people, so keep trying until you find one that works. Among the most popular protective techniques are:

1. **Performing a Ritual Bath:** This is a great way to purify both the aura and the physical body. It is also a way to bring in good, loving energy. I recommend you perform one of these baths at least once a month or more often if you feel the need. Use the time to meditate while you are in the water and say a prayer before entering and exiting the bath. You'll need a large bowl or container of water, some sacred oil, and a candle to start this. Begin by lighting the candle, and then take your time to run your bath and light a little incense. When the water is ready, slowly enter the bath without splashing. Begin to relax and allow the water to flow over you. Keep your eyes closed as you lower yourself into the water. Let as much energy flow through as possible, and do not be afraid to completely let go if it feels right for you. When you are ready to get out, slowly ease yourself out of the water and climb onto the towel or mat. After you have finished your bath, avoiding contact with other people is advisable until after communicating with the angels because their energy can interfere with your

cleanse.

2. **Creating an Energy Field:** This protective shield can be created by performing a meditation where you draw in positive and negative energy and create your own personal shield around yourself. If you are feeling disoriented or off-balance, this is also a great way to tone down your aura so that it is not so strong and overpowering. For angelic encounters, it is best to have this shield of protection around you at all times instead of just creating it when you need it.

3. **Using Crystals:** Crystals are wonderful tools to use for protection. They can help to maintain a flow of energy and block unwanted energies from entering your energy field. In addition to this, they can also keep different spiritual energies from interfering with each other. Some of the most common crystals used for protection include onyx, black obsidian, clear quartz, pyrite, black tourmaline, and amethyst.

4. **Visualization:** Visualization is a great way to enhance your spiritual protection. Visualizing an energy field around yourself can help maintain a buffer of protection that will keep negative energies from entering your aura field.

5. **Cleansing Your Space:** Cleaning your home and removing clutter from your life is a way to create more space for positive energy in your life. The less clutter you have in your home, the more energy you'll have for yourself. It may be time to clean out some of those stuffed closets and remove things you no longer need or want. This is a great way to increase your aura's clarity. You can also smoke your space with herbs like sage, incense, or palo santo.

This is not a complete list of all the ways to increase your spiritual protection. It's important to keep trying different techniques until you find one that works for you. As we get older and our worldview changes, we may also have to adjust what we use for protection. Finding what works for you is a process of trial and error, but this could also help you to discover new techniques that will work better.

Ultimately, it is not just about what techniques we use but how we use them. Having the right intention behind our actions is just as important as how we act. The more we can be at peace with ourselves internally, the better chance we can connect with angels. An angel's job is to help us maintain a state of mental, emotional, and spiritual balance, so the more we keep our intentions pure and in harmony with the universe, the easier it will be for them to come through. In addition to this, we should also work on building more positive energy into our lives by doing things that are good for us. This will help increase the positive energy around us and consequently attract angels that want to help us maintain this balance. Now that we have covered protection and set the stage, let us get down to business by considering some ways to make contact with angels.

Establishing a Line of Communication

The idea of communication with an angelic being is quite mystical, especially if you are not a believer in spiritual beings. This is perfectly understandable because no matter how much we understand the universe, there is still much more to learn and explore. However, some very simple steps can be taken to increase your chances of having a positive experience while searching for angels.

First and foremost, it is important to keep an open mind because if you do not, you are only setting yourself up for failure. After all, most of us have been taught to dismiss things we do not understand, which can lead to some very closed-minded thinking. Having an open mind involves being ready to consider all the possibilities, not just the ones we are comfortable with. With an open mind, you are more likely to see the truth and not be afraid of it. When you have an open mind, angelic communication is much more likely because it is only *after we are certain* that something is possible that we can invoke angels. Letting go of anxiety and being willing to explore new things is a great way to increase your chances of connecting with beings from other worlds.

Another thing that you can do to increase your chances of making contact with angels is to spend time in nature. I would recommend spending time outdoors in nature and going on frequent walks. This will help you relax and clear your mind so that you can listen to what the universe is telling you. Nature is a place where we can feel the presence of God, and this connection is something to cherish. Some people find it easier to connect with angels when they take long, hot baths or spend time meditating alone in their home, but you may want to give nature a try as well.

Finally, get rid of all distractions because this will help create an atmosphere conducive to reaching out and making contact with a spiritual being. If you want to make angelic contact, you must be completely focused on the task. It can be nearly impossible to achieve this if you are surrounded by a lot of noise and chaos in your life. The less clutter in your mind, the better chance you have at opening yourself up fully to what the universe is trying to tell you.

One of the most important things that you can do to increase your chances of connecting with angels is to be happy. This is not just an idle statement either, as it is easy to assume that we will quickly be able to attract happy spirits into our life if we are only blessed with happiness itself. The reality is that it takes a great deal of effort to maintain happiness in your life. It is not something that comes easily but involves working at making yourself happier. You can work at doing this in many ways, and the most important is by setting intentions. You can set an intention to be happy, healthy, at peace, or whatever you want to create in your life.

You may believe that you must put in a lot of hard work to find your angels. However, it is important to realize that achieving happiness only takes a bit of intention and hard work each day. You do not have to spend the rest of your life working on yourself because once you have made it, wellness will become a permanent part of your life. It is not something that you have to struggle with, and it is also not something that is going to go away. In the same way that a master chef can prepare a delicious meal in minutes, taking only minutes each day to focus on making yourself happy is enough to improve your health and wellness.

I mentioned earlier that there are many ways that you can make contact with angels, but we will focus on two specific cases, meditating on the angelic realm and getting an angel reading. Both of these are methods for reaching out to angels and making them more available for you.

How Can You Communicate?

Meditation: There are many forms of meditation, with the most popular being Transcendental Meditation. TM is a technique that involves you sitting relaxed with your eyes closed and focusing on breathing from your belly. Your focus is on one object, and your thought processing should be kept to a minimum at all times. When you meditate, it is vitally important not to try to control the content of your thoughts because if you do, you'll be focusing on yourself and not the entity you are connecting with.

One of the things that you can do to find more information about meditation is by reading what other people have had to say about it. This is a great way to get tips on meditation techniques that work best for you, and it is also a way of increasing your own understanding of the techniques. Meditation has proven time and time again to provide benefits of all kinds, including better stress management, overall improvement in life, and even better health.

Pendulum Reading: This is a form of angelic reading. There are many different types of pendulums with varying styles and purposes. Pendulums can be used in many ways ranging from simple pendulum magic to very complex rituals involving spells and rituals. The purpose of using a pendulum is to relay information that you would typically not be able to get by first-hand observation only. You ask the question, and then the pendulum goes into action, indicating the answer. This is a great way to discover who your guides are and how they want you to move forward.

Pendulums can be used to find out if someone is preventing you from moving forward in life or whether it is only a matter of direction. Pendulums can even be used to try and guess the kind of work you are meant to be doing in life. If a pendulum gives you a number, it is up to you to decide how this number relates back to reality.

If you are unfamiliar with pendulums, try finding one that feels right. A pendulum can be any item that is on a string or cord, such as a ring, crystal, or wood. Choose an object that has special meaning to you and holds some of your own energy. Hold it in your hands and allow yourself to become attuned to its energy. When you are ready, sit quietly, close your eyes, and reach out with all of your senses, seeking any vibrations from the Angelic Realm. Focus on every sensation and feeling you experience as if it is something of great importance. After 5 to 10 minutes, take the pendulum out, and you'll be ready to start getting answers to the questions you have in your mind.

If you are a beginner at this, it is best to keep things simple and connect with one or two energies rather than connecting with every angel that may be around. If you try and do this all at once without guidance, it will not work well for you at all. The interpretation of the pendulum's movements must be agreed upon before any communication begins. For instance, you can tell the pendulum to swing forward for **YES** and backward for **NO**, or vice versa, i.e., backward for yes, and forward for no. Now, wait for the pendulum to respond in agreement with your request, and if the pendulum swings back and forth between each request, you are on the right track. If not, give it a few minutes and try again.

Once you have agreed on how to interpret the movements of your pendulum, begin asking questions. You can ask basic yes or no questions at first, such as, "Is anyone here with me?", "Am I doing this right?" or "Is this the right time to ask these questions?" If you do not receive any response, then stop using your pendulum and try again later. With practice, you will be able to proceed to more complicated questions.

Tarot Cards: The tarot is an ancient divination and fortune-telling tool used by many people across the world. It can effectively reach out to your angels and receive answers to questions you may have. Some people find it easier to connect with their angels through tarot cards because the images are so clear and accessible in a way that many other forms of meditation are not. The connection you make with the card becomes a focal point that helps you begin receiving information from the angels.

Tarot cards can help you effectively reach out to your angels.

When using tarot cards, practice being present. Pay attention to everything you are experiencing as you try to interpret the images you see on the card through your senses. If a card shows a person, ask who is depicted in the image, how old they appear to be, and their role in your life. If there are symbols such as stars or masks, then begin to focus on their meanings. If the image shows a tree, then ask yourself what kind of tree it is and what it symbolizes for you. When you are ready, ask your angelic companions to give you answers to the questions that you have regarding the cards that you have seen.

Crystals and Gemstones: Crystal reading is a form of angelic communication that utilizes crystals and gemstones. Crystal readings are an excellent way to connect with your angels because they are versatile, illuminating, and beautiful. They help your angels to be able to speak directly to your mind, and you find that their answers come in quick-moving bursts of information in a flash. If you have not used stones or crystals before, you must begin by connecting with the crystal you selected before trying to go further.

Once you have found a crystal that works for you, then it is time to work on the technique. You need to close your eyes and imagine a figure representing the angel you are trying to communicate with in your mind's eye. Then, simply sit quietly and ask the spirit of your crystal to communicate with the angel you have asked it to try and reach. If you can, have your stone on hand or nearby to be within easy reach. The answers will come in any form which may be relevant to the person asking the questions. For some people, this may be through words or sentences, but for others, it might come in through a feeling or sensation. Sometimes the answers may not be in words or feelings but in an image or memory. The answers may also come as signs or symbols that have special meaning for the person asking them.

The best way to learn about crystals and gemstones is to find out what kind of experiences you have when you are with them. If, after a few weeks of trying, you discover more about yourself through the stones, then this is a good sign that you are on the right track with your communication.

Invoking an Angel

Invocation is another form of angelic communication which involves the summoning of an angel to help you through your problems. Invocation can be a powerful means of bringing about change in your life. However, it has some rules, rituals, and guidelines you should follow if you want to ensure that your message is received by the angels and not some other spirit or entity.

Step One: Begin by creating a ritual space where you can do this invocation safely and effectively. You can do this by turning off all the lights and lighting some candles, creating a sense of mystery and spirituality. Place any relevant crystals and gemstones on your altar, as well as any other items such as pictures or statues that help inspire your meditation. Select an area in your home where you feel most comfortable, such as a quiet room where you'll not be disturbed.

Step Two: Now, prepare yourself for the invocation. This can be done by washing your hands and face, wearing clean clothing, and fresh fragrant flowers that you have picked yourself. You then need to focus on the angels you want to communicate with. Take a moment to consider what it is that you need help with and why. Make a mental list of all of your concerns to form a coherent message for the angel in your mind's eye.

Step Three: Moving forward, you need to face your altar and begin to meditate. If you have been doing this practice before, you'll know what it feels like to have a vision of an angel standing right in front of you, although if you have never done it before, this is your chance to learn. Picture the angel in whatever way works best for you. Some people find it easier to visualize a small child, and some people use angels from the scriptures, although whichever way you do it, you need to be able to imagine clearly and vividly. It is important that you maintain contact with the angel by focusing on them, even if for just a few moments.

Step Four: When you feel that you have made the connection clearly, then ask for an answer to your concerns. When there is a reply, determine how well you can understand it. Often the answers come in symbols or images which require interpretation on your part. Take your time and try to figure out what the image or symbol means for you. Then cast a circle by drawing a sacred symbol on the floor in front of you, protecting against any harmful forces that may be trying to break in.

Chapter Seven: The Archangels of the Four Corners

The Jewish tradition teaches us that, to keep the world in order, God assigned four special angels the responsibility of watching the earth's four corners. Having such a task was not easy, and the angels were given special powers that would help them protect their designated corner. Michael, assigned to the South, was bestowed with the power of fire. Gabriel, the keeper of the West, was given control over the element of water. Raphael, who guards the East, was given charge of the wind. Finally, Uriel, who watches over the North, has command over the Earth. The Jewish prayer, Kriat Shema, written and read three times a day by all orthodox Jews, asks for protection from these four angels. The prayer contains the names of each angel associated with the element and corner of the Earth he guards. It is basically a call asking for Uriel's protection from the north, Raphael's from the east, Michael's from the south, and Gabriel's from the west.

The shamanic practice of calling on these four archangels was brought to Europe by Jewish refugees from Spain and Portugal who fled the mass exodus in 1492. The study and teaching of these four archangels are now widespread throughout all segments of Judaism (Orthodox Judaism) and to a lesser degree within all Indo-Aryan religions.

The belief that angels are at each of the four compass points can be found in numerous cultures worldwide, including Native American tradition. There are certain elements common to all of these traditions. The four cardinal directions, north, south, east, and west, were all considered special in the ancient world, and each is associated with its own unique deity. Each direction is considered the guardian of an element, which governs a specific sphere of human activity. In neo-paganism, this tradition is currently experiencing a renaissance, reflecting a growing interest in the esoteric traditions of our ancestors. In addition to the protection offered by these special angels in the east and west, time was divided into four seasons, each ruled by its own guardian, also known as an archangel. In Hebrew lore, Michael is the guardian of spring and summer, Gabriel is associated with autumn, Uriel is the guardian of winter, and Raphael presides over spring.

The four Cardinal Virtues (Temperance, Fortitude, Justice, and Prudence) are named after the four archangels. Our ancestors highly valued these virtues as a key to living an ethical life. God was known to embody these virtues, just as the four angels were known to watch over the cardinal points. Temperance was closely associated with Michael, Fortitude with Raphael, Justice with Gabriel, and Prudence with Uriel. While these virtues may not be well-known in popular culture, they are still part of our collective consciousness and are being taught in synagogues and schools worldwide.

Angels, like human beings, are themselves composed of various elemental parts. The four elements are:

- Earth (Geburah)
- Wind (Tehinnah)
- Water (Hod)
- Fire (Yesod)

These correspond to the physical body, emotions, ego, and intellect. Working together, these four make up our entire being. When each is not balanced with its corresponding element, it becomes imbalanced, causing disharmony and imbalance within our lives. When a person is unbalanced, it reflects in their lives.

Unbalanced emotions lead to destructive, even murderous behavior.

An unbalanced ego results in an inflated sense of self, which leads to violence and arrogance. An unbalanced intellect can result in betrayal and cruelty toward one's fellow man. The angelic guardians of the elements act as a balancer, restoring harmony and balance when one's element is unbalanced. With the imbalance of one of these elements can come illness, depression, fear, and hopelessness. The guardians of the elements are not there to cure these illnesses but rather to help restore order and balance.

In the Jewish tradition, the angels are also associated with the four worlds of existence, Atzilut, Briah, Yetzirah, and Assiah. When one achieves harmony within these four worlds, one will ascend to higher levels of spirituality, moving closer to God. This practice falls under the umbrella of Jewish mysticism and is considered to be an intermediate level between beginner and advanced practice.

The first documented association between Michael, Gabriel, Uriel, and Raphael with their respective elements was in an essay called "The Book of Life," written by Isha Schwaller De Lubicz. It took place in 1907 at the annual congress of occultists worldwide. In this essay, he described how each angel was associated with one or more of these elements. The idea was further developed in the 1940s by Samael Aun Weor, who wrote that the four elements and the four cardinal directions were spiritual forces resembling a circle's quadrants. They were responsible for creating an invisible whirling vortex within the universe.

Moving counterclockwise, they created a continuous cycle of manifestation, creation, preservation, destruction, and dissolution. They were also believed to contain a fifth element, which was the "Tetragrammaton" or "Sha-He-Vau-He," the sacred name of God. This is the source of all life, and it is recounted in Genesis as one of only four letters needed to construct the universe. The five-pointed star is a symbol of these five elements. In the Jewish tradition, this symbol is called "The Shield of David" and is one of the most prominent symbols of Judaism, along with the menorah. It is a reminder that there is only one God (Sha-He-Vau-He).

Archangel Michael, Guardian of the South

In the western tradition, the symbols associated with Michael are the eagle and the color red. The eagle is a symbol of transformation and selflessness. In Freemasonry, it is considered to be a symbol of immortality and rebirth. In alchemy, it represents fire and thus transformation.

Fire was considered by our ancestors to be an essential element in life and was believed to hold all potential within its transformative power. Michael is the guardian of the element of fire, known as Geburah. The color red symbolizes fire's creative and destructive power, associated with its fiery nature. It is a symbol of war, violence, and rage. However, when it is balanced, it can be associated with selflessness, courage, and strength.

In the Bible, Michael is said to have appeared in front of the prophet Daniel to help him understand a vision he had seen. He also appeared before King Solomon to help him choose between two women who claimed to be the same child's mother. In Islam, he is known as "Jibril" and is one of the seven angels standing before God's throne. He is a warrior angel who has been sent to defend the faithful as a commander of God's army against evil. The Qur'an informs us that he revealed to Mohammed the location of Paradise and Hell. He is represented by a sword and a pair of wings, symbolizing his role as one who carries death but also medicine and life.

In the qabalah, Michael represents Gevurah, one of the ten sephirot on the Tree of Life. Gevurah carries a variety of meanings in Hebrew, ranging from restraint, strength, and power. Also associated with the element of fire, it is considered to be a force that is necessary for the balancing of all other forces. Thus, Michael is referred to as being "the prince of peace" since he brings an understanding of the law by helping one reconcile with oneself and one's own internal conflicts. He represents the ability to come to terms with hard facts in life and not act out on impulse.

- **Color:** Michael is most associated with the color red, which is known as the color of fire. The color red also symbolizes strength, vigor, and passion. In Freemasonry, blue is associated with Michael. Blue is seen as an emblem of light, purity, and constancy. In Christianity, it is symbolic of heaven and immortality. Green is also associated with Michael because he represents nature.

- **Chakras:** The chakras of Michael are said to be in the pituitary, adrenal and solar plexus. The pituitary is associated with ego-consciousness, the adrenal with emotions and passions, and the solar plexus with instinctual energy. Each of these three areas has a chakra at each point. The hormones associated with these areas impact our behavior and reactions to situations. Michael is said to help provide balance when they are imbalanced.

- **Planets:** Michael is associated with Saturn because he is the guardian of the element of Geburah. According to ancient astrology, Saturn's influence was thought to bring about a greater understanding of reality and a gradual change in consciousness. The color associated with Saturn is red-gold.

- **Sun Signs:** Michael is associated with the sun sign Leo. As one of the three fixed signs of the zodiac, Leo is known as the sign of self-expression and ego. It is also a fire sign.

- **Vibration:** Truth, authenticity, and selflessness.

- **Crystals:** Blue sapphire, golden labradorite, sodalite, and lapis lazuli are crystals that can be used to help ground Michael's energy.

- **Symbols:** The symbol of Michael is a golden eagle with wings spread – a symbol of protection and regeneration.

- **Invocation Tip:** The best time to invoke Michael is during the summer months at 11:11 a.m. and 11:11 p.m. When invoking Michael to help put you in a state of receptivity for his energy and messages, it is helpful to contemplate the symbology associated with Michael, such as the eagle.

Archangel Gabriel, Guardian of the West

Gabriel is known as the messenger angel, who symbolizes communication and the regulation of our interaction with others. In the Christian tradition, he is most well-known for bringing the messages of God to both humans and angels. His name means "God is my strength," which is a positive quality associated with him. He represents God's power, which is evident in his name, "Gabriel," which means "God's hero." In Islam, he brought news of God's revelation to Mohammed and instructed Daniel on how long the exile would be. He is associated with the color green, which symbolizes the growth of life. He has the power to reveal divine light and is considered to be a healer and teacher who helps us grow spiritually.

In Qabalah, Gabriel represents Keter. Keter means "the crown" and is one of ten sephirot on the Tree of Life. As the crown, it sustains creation as it evolves through its many cycles of manifestation. It is also associated with God's ability to create without limit or bounds and with His ability to permeate all creation and everything in it by His divine breath (Vau). Thus, it is associated with inhalation, inspiration, and resurrection. Considered the angel of mercy and love, Gabriel helps us develop these qualities in our lives and grow. "*The angel who unites the Creator with all created things, who mediates between heaven and earth*" is how Rabbi Shlomo Yitzchaki described him.

- **Color:** Gabriel is associated with the color green, which symbolizes growth and renewal.

- **Chakras:** The chakras of Gabriel are in the crown and throat. The throat represents our ability to communicate, and Gabriel's role as the messenger of God means that he can help us learn how to speak clearly and effectively, as well as make our voice an instrument for good.

- **Planets:** Gabriel is associated with Uranus. Uranus is a planet that represents the discovery of our true nature. It can be seen as a struggle between two opposing forces, the desire for freedom and individuality and the need for security and community. It is associated with many colors, including green, purple, blue, yellow, black, and musical notes.

- **Sun Signs:** Gabriel is associated with Aquarius because of his association with Uranus. Aquarius is thought to represent strong individuality, the liberation of self-expression, and a new dawning of consciousness. It also represents an individual's ability to remain independent of outside influence, which can be contrary to desire or necessity.

- **Vibration:** Truth, love, and abundance.

- **Crystals:** Green sodalite and lapis lazuli are crystals that can be used to help ground Gabriel's energy.

- **Symbols:** The symbol of Gabriel is a two-winged angel with a trumpet. The two wings represent his role as a messenger of God, and the trumpet represents the message he brings.

- **Invocation Tip:** To invoke Gabriel's energy, meditating on the symbols and colors associated with him is useful. It is also useful to find a green object or a picture of a green-winged angel and place it where you'll see it frequently. When in prayer, you can invoke his energy by calling upon him to help you communicate effectively, making your voice an instrument of good and delivering messages from God.

Archangel Raphael, Guardian of the East

Raphael is the messenger angel of healing who brings us divine knowledge. He is associated with the color purple, which symbolizes the power of healing and wholeness. His name means "God has healed," and this healing quality has favored him greatly during his long association with humanity. He is associated with compassion, mercy, and unconditional love (Rah). In the bible, God tasked him with ministering to the Israelites after their exodus from Egypt, and he assisted Tobias in his journey back to his homeland. He also assisted Abraham in crossing the Red Sea. He exemplifies patience, persistence, and self-control as a role model for humanity. His healing role is reflected in his association with Venus, the planet of love and attraction.

In Qabalah, Raphael represents Chokmah. Chokmah is the second sephira on the Tree of Life and is associated with wisdom. It represents the active side of knowledge and experience. It is considered to contain everything that exists in potential, including all opposites in their perfect balance, as well as being able to give birth without limit or bounds. Thus, it is associated with inspiration, the breath of life, and resurrection. Raphael helps us grow spiritually through his healing qualities and compassion for humanity. He can help us become more introspective and sensitive to the problems of others so that we can better understand their issues from a compassionate point of view.

- **Colors:** Purple is the color of healing, and Raphael's role as the angel of healing means that he can help us become sensitive to and receptive to his healing influence.

- **Chakras:** The chakra of Raphael is in the heart, representing our compassion and ability to love others.

- **Planets:** Raphael is associated with Venus. Venus is a planet that represents love, refinement, and attraction, and these qualities represent his healing energy.

- **Sun Signs:** Raphael is associated with Taurus because he is associated with Venus. Taurus is known for its steadfastness and perseverance in working toward its goals, which reflects Raphael's desire for humanity to continue working toward spiritual perfection.

- **Vibration:** Forgiveness, health, and joy.

- **Crystals:** Amethyst and jadeite can be used to cleanse and open up Raphael's subtle energy centers.

- **Symbols:** The symbol of Raphael is a purple circular disk surrounded by angelic wings.

- **Invocation Tip:** When preparing for a healing session is the best time to invoke Archangel Raphael.

Archangel Uriel, Guardian of the North

Uriel means "God is my light," and his name symbolizes the integration of spirit and matter. He has aided humanity in its spiritual evolution since the early days of creation, when he is said to have helped Noah build the ark after the great flood. In Egypt, he was the leader of a group of angels who protected and helped humans while Pharaoh enslaved them. He also helped Moses to escape Egypt with the Israelite people.

In Qabalah, Uriel represents Netzach. Netzach is one of ten sephirot on the Tree of Life and is associated with our ability to suffer or endure earthly existence to fulfill our goals. It is also associated with attraction, restoration, and renewal. Uriel, who aids spiritual evolution, can help us in our personal spiritual growth through his ability to help us endure suffering and life's challenges. He can also help us to regain our strength and resolve, through which we can achieve our goals.

- **Colors:** Yellow is the color of Netzach and is associated with Uriel's tranquility and wisdom.
- **Chakras:** The chakras of Uriel are in the throat and third eye. The throat represents communication, which is an important part of spiritual awakening. The third eye represents our ability to see beyond the physical world into a higher plane of consciousness.
- **Planets:** Uriel is associated with Jupiter. Jupiter is a planet that indicates expansion, relationship, and stability, and these qualities represent his healing energy. It is also associated with many colors such as yellow, blue, red, green, white, and violet (light blue).
- **Sun Signs:** Uriel is associated with Gemini. Gemini is known for its quick and adaptable mind, which attributes to the importance of communication during spiritual growth. He is also associated with Aquarius because of his association with Uranus. Aquarius is known for their detached sense of individuality, freedom, and change, which reflects his role as a guide in our spiritual evolution.
- **Vibration:** Truth, faith, and higher purpose.
- **Crystals:** Smoky quartz or yellow calcite can help activate

Uriel's energy in the subtle bodies.

- **Symbols:** The symbol for Uriel is a blue circular disk surrounded by rays of gold.

- **Invocation Tip:** You may feel Uriel's presence in the middle of meditation or quiet contemplation when you are on the verge of opening up to another level of consciousness.

Chapter Eight: More Archangels and How to Work with Them

Archangel Azrael

In western tradition, the symbols associated with Azrael are a cup and a scythe. The cup symbolizes introspection and reflection, while the scythe represents transformation. The cup represents Christ's words in Christianity: *"I came not to bring peace but a sword."* This statement was meant to show that we must fight our own inner demons to be able to make spiritual progress along our path.

The scythe is an instrument that is used in harvesting crops and reaping death, especially through war or pestilence. It is a symbol of death but also of transition and renewal. According to alchemy, the scythe represents aging and renewal. Azrael is often called the angel of death since his duty is to bear the souls of the dead and guide them into their new life.

He is also described as being associated with Saturn, which in ancient astrology was thought to represent an inner strength or maturity that produced a change in one's consciousness. The power attributed to both Saturn and Azrael has been considered necessary to make progress on one's path toward enlightenment.

In Buddhism, Amitabha Buddha is portrayed holding either a cup or a jewel in his hand. This is about Azrael, who is considered Amitabha's attendant.

In the Kabbalah, Azrael is associated with the sephirah Binah. Binah is known as the mother of the universe and is representative of understanding and wisdom. It represents a personal relationship with God and a sense of trust in God's care for oneself. Azrael also represents the eleventh hour of Malkuth, which means to be an expression of divine power in the physical world. As such, he can also represent time, especially that which has elapsed since one's birth or rebirth into this life.

- **Color:** Azrael is associated with the color black. Black symbolizes power, authority, and judgment. According to Hinduism and Buddhism, it represents death.

- **Chakras:** The chakras of Azrael are in the heart, throat, third eye, crown chakra, and base chakra.

- **Planets:** Azrael is associated with the planet Saturn. This planet's association with time has made it an appropriate choice for this angelic representative since Azrael serves as the custodian of time during one's entire life span on Earth. As such, he represents the law of karma and destiny as well as divine justice and divine mercy that attends us throughout our lifetime. The color associated with this planet is silver-white.

- **Sun Signs:** Azrael is associated with the sun sign Scorpio. Scorpio is known as the sign of regeneration, death, rebirth, and transformation. Because this sign is a water sign, it has a deep connection to the unconscious mind and to psychic processes. This connection has led others to associate it with magic and sorcery. Azrael is also associated with the sun sign Sagittarius. Sagittarius is known as the archer and represents directness, honesty, and freedom of expression. It also represents an ability to see a situation from many perspectives, which can help one understand truth and make wise decisions based upon that understanding. The color associated with this sun sign is gold.

- **Vibration:** Light, wisdom, and inner change.

- **Crystals:** Black obsidian, jasper, chrysoberyl, and red garnet are crystals that can be used to help ground Azrael's energy.

- **Symbols:** The symbol of Azrael is a scythe and cup. As stated above, this represents the reaping of death through war or pestilence while also representing the reaping of death through natural forces such as aging, disease, and death itself. Azrael's symbol is also a feather. Feathers have been used to help connect the earthly realm with that of angels by providing a medium for transmitting messages. In Hinduism, the word for feather is said to be *aksa,* representing the power of flight. It also represents the power of inner awareness as well as spiritual aspirations. Feathers also represent wisdom and spiritual power in many Native American tribes. In Aztec culture, Azrael is referred to as The Feathered Serpent and depicted with talons and feathers adorning his body. The Feathered Serpent represents life, death, rebirth, and evolution through a transformation because it sheds its skin every few years.

- **Invocation Tip:** The best time to invoke Azrael is during the fall. He can also be invoked during new moon rituals. It is helpful to contemplate the symbology of Azrael when invoking him to help put you in a state of receptivity for his energy and messages.

Archangel Chamuel

Chamuel is known as the angel of love and compassion. His name means "He that sees God" and refers to his ability to simultaneously see the past, present, and future. Chamuel acts as an envoy of God's love so humanity may achieve spiritual progress by dealing with its darker passions. He is one of the angels who preside over Taurus's zodiac sign, characterized by its reliability and perseverance or tenacity. It is represented by the element Earth, which symbolizes stability and dependability. Taurus also represents those things that are tangible and physical and is associated with body and matter.

Chamuel has a healing effect on human consciousness, especially with understanding how negative emotions can be transformed into positive energy. As a representative of introspection, he helps us transform our internal emotional life and our relationship with others while helping us understand how we can heal emotional wounds that have occurred in past lives and in this lifetime. He can help heal and transform the heart, enabling it to be more open to love and wholeness. As the angel of love, he works with Archangel Sandalphon to form the angelic order of archangels known as the Elohim. He is exalted above all creatures in his knowledge of God and his power to heal human suffering.

Chamuel's positive energy can have a powerful healing effect on ailments related to the respiratory system (i.e., asthma, bronchitis) and those related to hormone production (i.e., infertility and impotence). Those who work with Chamuel often find their ability to manifest wealth at all levels greatly enhanced. Chamuel's energy can also help one work through the more difficult parts of past lives to attain a greater sense of peace and spiritual wholeness. As the angel of peace, he teaches one how to achieve inner peace and balance during difficult circumstances.

- **Colors:** White, purple, and gold.

- **Chakras:** The chakras of Chamuel are in the heart, head, solar plexus, and third eye.

- **Planets:** Chamuel is associated with the planet Mercury. This planet is associated with communication, intellect, mental function, education, and learning. It also represents a higher spiritual life, which is highly connected to the power of intuition. The color associated with this planet is silver-white.

- **Sun Signs:** Chamuel is associated with the sun sign Taurus.

- **Vibration:** Compassion, understanding, and transformation.

- **Crystals:** The Herkimer diamond is a crystal that works well with Chamuel.

- **Symbols:** Chamuel's symbol is a caduceus or staff with two serpents wrapped around it. He is often depicted holding a branch in his left hand, which represents the healing of physical ailments through the power of compassion. The other two snakes are symbolic of healing the wounds of the past.

- **Invocation Tip:** The best time to invoke Chamuel is during the winter solstice and during new moon rituals. He can also be invoked during planetary transits such as Mercury, Venus, and Mars.

Archangel Raguel

Raguel's name means "friend of God." He is known as the guardian angel of the planet Earth and represents divine justice. He is believed to be the guide of souls who pass through the underworld on their way to heaven. Like a guardian angel, he works with both humans and animals. Sometimes, he is depicted with animal heads, for example, a dog or a lion. In these forms, his function can also be seen as that of a protector and messenger between heaven and earth. Raguel helps us discover our divine will according to what we need in our spiritual path so that we might find increased happiness while fulfilling our own unique mission. Raguel's energy is also closely allied to that of Chamuel in that he helps us learn how to use our emotions positively and how to overcome their negative expressions in our lives. He teaches us how to deal with anger, hatred, lust, and other worldly desires to find greater peace within ourselves. In addition, he teaches us how to radically accept love from the divine realm into our own lives because of the spiritual power it holds for self-awareness.

In the Bible, Raguel is mentioned in the book of Isaiah. He appears as a prophet who witnesses the destruction of Babylon and participates in Jesus' coming into the world. The symbol of Raguel depicts the beaded cord he carries around his neck, which is the mark of his prophetic mission and divine authority. As a prophet, he often has a relationship with God on behalf of humanity. He may also be given assignments to protect and defend particular people or places.

In the qabalah, Raguel is the archangel of the sephirah of Netzach. The sephirah Netzach is associated with emotions, instincts, and the force that unites thought with action. His symbol is two overlapping triangles, one pointing up and the other pointing down. This symbol represents the union of heaven and earth as well as the union of matter with spirit. Netzach also represents those things that come into being through conflict. It is connected to feelings, desires as well as sexuality, and secret passions.

- **Colors:** Blue, gray, and silver.

- **Chakras:** The chakras of Raguel are the heart, throat, solar plexus, and third eye.

- **Planets:** Raguel is associated with the planet Uranus which is linked to abstract ideas, freedom, and autonomy. It can also be associated with creativity, metaphysics, science fiction, extraterrestrials, and technology. Raguel is also linked to the planet Mercury, known for communication and intellect. The color of this planet is silver-white.

- **Sun Signs:** Raguel is associated with the sun sign Gemini.

- **Vibration:** Peace, understanding, and transformation.

- **Crystals:** Citrine, aquamarine, and carnelian

- **Symbols:** Raguel's symbol is a staff or wand with letters on it that spell out his name in Hebrew letters and his title, "friend of God," as well as an eye in the middle. The staff, which serves as a symbol of the divine, is related to justice and protection. The letters which spell his name in Hebrew on the staff's shaft remind us that we must be willing to speak up for what is right. The eye at the center of the staff represents knowledge, purity, and God's watchful presence.

- **Invocation Tip:** The best time to invoke Raguel is during the winter solstice and the waxing moon. Invoking him on Mondays, Wednesdays, and Fridays is also good. He can also be invoked during planetary transits such as Uranus, Mercury, and Venus.

Archangel Zadkiel

Zadkiel is the archangel of freedom, mercy, forgiveness, and gratitude. Often depicted with a sword in his hand or a sword sheathed at his side, he is said to be the highest angel of grace. In addition, he is seen holding grapes or ears of wheat in his hand to represent divine nourishment for the soul. Zadkiel's role can also be seen as that of a teacher who guides us on our spiritual path and encourages us to embrace God's gift of universal love, divine forgiveness, and spirituality within our daily lives. He can be invoked to help us to understand how the past governs our present lives and how we are always connected to the divine realm.

In the qabalah, Zadkiel is the archangel of the sephirah Binah. Binah is associated with understanding and enlightenment. It is related to thought, intelligence, and memory. Zadkiel's symbol is a crown with two cobwebs, representing divine illumination. In addition, the sephirah of Binah also represents divine action and purpose.

- **Colors:** Violet
- **Chakras:** The chakras of Zadkiel are the heart, throat, and third eye.
- **Planets:** Zadkiel is associated with the planet Jupiter, known for growth, expansion, abundance, and good fortune. Jupiter's color is yellow-gold.
- **Sun Signs:** Zadkiel is associated with the sun sign of Libra, representing balance and harmony as well as relationships and love. He is also associated with Sagittarius.
- **Vibration:** Spiritual connection, mercy, and charity.
- **Crystals:** Clear quartz crystal.
- **Symbols:** Zadkiel is often depicted with a sword. The symbol of the sword represents divine protection. It also represents the divine power that frees us from our own ignorance and arrogance to embrace divine wisdom, love, and sympathy for others.

- **Invocation Tip:** The best time to invoke Zadkiel is during the winter solstice when the light comes into the world. It is good to invoke him on Mondays, Wednesdays, and Fridays. It may also be good to invoke him during planetary transits such as Jupiter, Uranus, and Mercury.

Archangel Jophiel

Jophiel is the archangel of wisdom, purity, and love. He is associated with the feminine aspects of the divine realm because he is often depicted as an angelic maiden. His presence can be felt in the ascent of the soul to the heights of self-awareness, spiritual power, and transcendence. He can be invoked to help us to understand how we can move beyond the search for knowledge toward a greater understanding of ourselves and how we are pure equals in divinity. In the Kabbalah, Jophiel is the archangel of Chokmah. Chokmah is associated with divine intelligence, intuition, and awareness. Its symbol is a flowing river that represents creative inspiration. This sephirah also represents our connection to the world of ideas.

- **Colors:** Yellow and green
- **Chakras:** The chakras of Jophiel are the heart, solar plexus, and third eye.
- **Planets:** Jophiel is associated with the planet Venus, which is associated with creativity, love, and happiness. It plays an important role in relationships and can also be linked to the element of water. Its color is yellow-green.
- **Sun Signs:** Jophiel is associated with the sun sign of Cancer, known for sensitivity, love, and compassion. He is also associated with the sun sign Scorpio, which is known for power, leadership, and sexuality.
- **Vibration:** Pure love, knowledge, and self-awareness.
- **Crystals:** Kyanite and amethyst crystals can be used to work with Jophiel.

- **Symbols:** Jophiel's symbol consists of three dots or circles which spell out his name in Hebrew letters and his title, "friend of God," in English. At the front of this symbol are two wings representing spiritual illumination and empathic understanding of others.

- **Invocation Tip:** The best time to invoke Jophiel is during the spring equinox when the light of the divine realm comes into the world. It is also good to invoke him on Mondays, Wednesdays, and Fridays, but he can be invoked at any time.

Chapter Nine: Prayers and Meditation

Prayer is a form of communication with God or any spiritual entity. Prayers can be as short as one word, but they can also be very long and detailed. It allows us to ask for help, give thanks, connect with someone or something in spiritual or emotional ways, and get closer to God. Prayer is universal. It is practiced by many faiths and cultures in many languages and styles.

Meditation is a time to calm your mind, focus on one thing, and become more aware of your environment and self. It can be practiced as a daily routine or used as a tool for healing, relaxation, or personal insight. Meditation allows us to focus our minds on one thing at a time, rather than being bombarded with external stimuli like other sounds or people. Focusing inward and being aware of our bodies, thoughts, and feelings may help us gain insight into who we are as human beings and enable us to reach angels for assistance.

Much of what we need in our lives comes from the universe, but how do we ask for it without sounding silly or naïve? The answer is prayer and meditation. Not only does it help us to better express ourselves, but it also helps us to connect with God and the angels on a deeper level. It is a way to acknowledge the source of all our needs and let them know that we want whatever they have to offer that could be useful to us.

Prayer to Archangel Michael

This prayer is best said on Sunday, the day dedicated to the Archangel Michael. The prayer will begin with an acknowledgment of the angel and gratitude for all he does. Then, pray to ask the archangel for his divine protection, strength, guidance, and wisdom in all aspects of your life. Ask him to be with you as you begin the new week and grant you the strength and courage to face the week's challenges. Ask for protection from all evil entities and request blessings upon yourself, your family, and all people. The prayer should end with gratitude as if your requests have already been granted. Use a few moments of silence to ground yourself before concluding the prayer.

Prayer to Archangel Gabriel

Monday is dedicated to the Archangel Gabriel, and this prayer would be best said on that day. This prayer asks for the archangel's divine protection and energy to help you bring joy, beauty, and happiness into your life. Ask him to guide you through the work week so that you may find peace and happiness within yourself. Request that he help you clear negative thoughts, energies, or people out of your life so that joy may continue to flow into your life. End the prayer with gratitude and praise, as if your request has already been granted. A few seconds of silence is ideal for grounding yourself before going about your day.

Prayer to Archangel Uriel

Tuesday is dedicated to Archangel Uriel, so this prayer should be said on that day. This prayer is for those who may feel unsure about their direction in life or their future. Ask for Uriel's divine protection and assistance, as well as his guidance and wisdom, so you may gain clarity about your future path. If you are struggling with a particular aspect of your life, ask for his help to release it from your life so that you can move forward in the most positive way possible. Acknowledge his presence in your life, then end the prayer with gratitude and praise, feeling as if your request has already been granted.

Prayer to Archangel Raphael

Wednesday is dedicated to Archangel Raphael, so this prayer should be said on that day. This prayer is for those who are struggling with negative thoughts or people in their lives. Ask for Raphael's divine protection and wisdom as well as his guidance and assistance throughout your week so that you can be more receptive to joy, beauty, and happiness in your life. Ask for help releasing negative thoughts, energies, or people from your life so you may find peace and happiness within yourself. Acknowledge his presence in your life as well as his energy and blessings. End the prayer with gratitude, then allow a few moments of silence to ground yourself before concluding the prayer.

Prayer to Archangel Selaphiel

This prayer should be said on Thursday. The prayer is to ask Selaphiel to help you achieve a healthy balance of love and work. Ask for a balance of your heart, mind, and spirit and help balance your love life. You may also desire help balancing work and play to be more productive. Pray for his divine guidance in your personal relationships or with coworkers. You may also wish to pray for his guidance as you search for a life partner or if you are feeling lost and alone. The prayer will end with gratitude and praise, feeling as if your request is already granted before going about your day. Acknowledge his energy and guidance, as it will help to balance the forces of light and dark within your life.

Prayer to Archangel Raguel

Friday is dedicated to archangel Raguel, and the prayer should be said on that day. This prayer is for those who may feel restless, unfulfilled, or alone even though others surround them. Ask for Raguel's divine protection and assistance as well as his guidance and wisdom so that you may find inspiration and clarity about your life path. You may also need help finding your purpose or balance in your personal relationships and careers. The prayer will end with gratitude, acknowledging that your request has already been granted before going about your day. Acknowledge his presence in your life, as it will help to inspire you and keep you focused on achieving goals.

Prayer to Archangel Barachiel

This prayer should be said on Saturday. The prayer is to ask Barachiel for his divine protection, energy, and guidance during the weekend. Ask for protection from all evil entities and assistance to remove that which is not of the light from your life so that you may be inspired and guided to continue moving forward in your journey. You may also wish to pray for help regaining faith in yourself or others and help to resolve personal issues from your past, so you can move forward with a clean slate. The prayer will end with gratitude and praise, feeling as if your request has already been granted before going about your weekend.

The above examples of prayers to angels provide you with a basic template of what prayer to angels may look like. However, you must personalize this in a way relevant to your needs or desires. You can change the angel's name according to which day you are saying the prayer, or you can add or remove certain aspects of the prayer. Use what you believe will work best for you and fit into your lifestyle. The angels can be called upon at any time to help us achieve our goals and achieve peace within ourselves. We may receive divine inspiration and guidance when it is most needed through prayer. Allow the angels to work with you in whichever way suits your needs. Pray and be open to receiving the answers that you seek.

Other Helpful Prayers

Prayer to Overcome Addiction

You may pray for help in overcoming addiction to any substance or substance. Pray for the strength and endurance to overcome the addiction and the willpower to resist that substance. You may also wish to ask for help in dealing with feelings of shame, embarrassment, guilt, and self-loathing. Perceive yourself as strong and courageous in this struggle. Feel your power as you heal from a deep place inside of you. The angels and God are with you in this process. You can also ask Archangel Michael to help free you and your loved ones from addiction. The following steps can be followed for a meditative exercise to assist the process:

Step One: Relax your mind and body. Take a few deep breaths, tune into your body, and relax.

Step Two: Imagine the energy of addiction leaving your body. Feel it leaving your body, through the top of your head, and out through the bottom of your feet.

Step Three: Imagine a strong light surrounding you and falling like rain, completely covering you in the light. This image will help to neutralize any negative effects that the addiction may have on you.

Step Four: Thank God for this opportunity to heal and release yourself from this bondage.

Step Five: Let all past feelings of shame, embarrassment, or guilt fall away with the energy of this healing. You are forgiven. You are free. You have the power to change your life and heal yourself.

Step Six: Thank the angels and God for your freedom. You can add any other meditations or prayers to this exercise if you want, such as asking to have visions of your desired outcome of healing from addiction or asking for protection from the addiction in question.

Prayer to Overcome Negative Thought Patterns

You may pray for help to overcome negative thought patterns that seem to keep repeatedly playing in your mind, preventing you from experiencing peace of mind. Pray for the strength and endurance to overcome these thoughts, wisdom, and guidance so that they no longer control your life. Ask Archangel Raphael to help you replace the negative thoughts with positive thoughts. Pray for help in breaking the cycle of negativity in your life. You can use meditation to assist in the process of transforming this negative energy into positive energy. This can be done with the following steps:

Step One: Relax your mind and body. Take a few deep breaths, tune into your body, and relax.

Step Two: Focus on breathing in a way that allows you to relax more each time you inhale and relax more each time you exhale.

Step Three: Turn your attention to your thoughts and note and describe negative thoughts that keep coming into your mind.

Step Four: Using the above prayer to Archangel Raphael, ask him to help cleanse you of all negative energy so that these thoughts no longer control you. Ask him to help you see them for what they are, the past and not the future. Feel his divine light surrounding you, allowing you to see clearly with Divine guidance.

Step Five: Give gratitude for this opportunity for healing and release yourself from this bondage.

Prayer for Peace of Mind

You can pray for help in achieving peace of mind. Pray for the strength and endurance to overcome anxiety and stress. Ask Archangel Raziel to help you use your mind to create a peaceful, tranquil environment around you. Pray for help to eliminate the causes of anxiety. Ask Archangel Uriel to help you overcome your fears. Let the angels and God guide you as you make changes in your life that will manifest the peace you desire. Begin to feel peaceful, tranquil, and calm as you meditate on these prayers.

Step One: Relax and let go of all tension and anxiety.

Step Two: Tune into your heart center, feeling the peace that this place creates. Feel yourself becoming peaceful.

Step Three: Begin to think only positive thoughts about yourself and your life. You may also include positive thoughts about God, angels, and the universe. The more you concentrate on these thoughts, the more reality will begin to reflect them in your life.

Step Four: Breathe in and out calmly, feeling peace, filling your body with each breath. You may pray for help to achieve a peaceful mind, such as when dealing with the panic and anxiety you may feel when going through changes. Ask Archangel Uriel to help you achieve a peaceful state of mind during these experiences and support you during this time by helping you find positive, helpful, and constructive ways to deal with your anxiety.

Step Five: When you feel relaxed enough, thank the angels for their help and conclude your exercise.

Prayer for Love in Your Life

You can pray for help in finding your true love and happiness. Pray for the strength, courage, and strength to find the qualities of love you seek. Ask Archangel Uriel to help you use your mind to create a deep, abiding sense of love and trust in your life. Pray for extra help and guidance as you work toward this goal. You can use meditation to help you achieve this with the following steps:

Step One: Relax your mind and body. Take a few deep breaths, tune into your body, and relax.

Step Two: Focus on breathing in a way that allows you to relax more each time you inhale and exhale.

Step Three: Imagine love flowing into your heart center. Feel it filling your heart center with love and kindness.

Step Four: Ask the angels to fill your heart center with unconditional love. Ask them to help you feel connected to all people and things around you. Allow the divine light of love to surround you, protecting you against anything that is not conducive to bringing out the best in all people and things.

Step Five: Give thanks for this opportunity to heal and release yourself from this burden of loneliness.

Chapter Ten: Working with Spirit Guides beyond Archangels

In the past, up until recently, most people focused on worshiping gods and goddesses from other cultures. These deities visited people through visions and dreams that priests and shamans interpreted. Most religions overlooked the spiritual power in everyone's hearts and focused on external objects such as statues reminiscent of gods to help people learn about the divine. The issue with this is that many people looking for a spiritual experience found themselves shut out by the traditional limitations of religion and spirituality. Now they turn to less mainstream practices, and with a little guidance, anyone can explore the benefits of spirituality outside the more traditional concepts of angels, gods, and goddesses.

Most people are familiar with angels as heavenly entities who serve as helpers on Earth in various ways, but not everyone is aware that departed loved ones, ancestors, ascended masters, or elementals can also work as spirit guides. Many people find these other types of spirit guides appealing for one reason or another. As with traditional angelic guides, most of these other non-angelic spirit guides are accessible to everyone, and what they have to offer may help you with your spiritual quest. The type of guide you get is based on your own beliefs and practices, but here are some common types of spirit guides that you may contact to get started:

Communicating with Your Ancestors

The ancestors of ancient times were much more in touch with nature and the worlds beyond than we are now. They learned early on to work with spirits of nature and passed that knowledge down through the generations. Today, many people are looking for ways to reconnect with their inner knowledge, and as a way to do so, many of these practitioners turn to their ancestors.

For some, communicating with their ancestors is as easy as talking to a family member who has passed. For others, it is a serious ritual in which the practitioner makes a special connection with his or her ancestors. In this ritual, you can expect to see visions or visit other dimensions with your ancestors as you ask for help and guidance in your life. When you honor your heritage, you acknowledge that you are part of a larger family. By being yourself as a spiritual being and merging with the higher vibrations, you can tap into the infinite wisdom within your ancestors.

Communicating with your ancestors can be as easy or as complex as you let it be. It is best to use the tools of meditation, visualization, and guided imagery to stay connected with those who have passed on. They can also help you interpret people, places, and events around you. Your ancestors are there to support you in your life, but they do not always have all the answers. They are here to help you develop the wisdom and discernment to live the life you want on this plane.

You can set up a special shrine in your home where you can regularly meditate or simply remain in contact with these guides. It is important to remember that ancestral spirits are not guiding you from beyond the grave but rather from the very source of life within you, so they are more than willing to help guide you through the process of learning and self-discovery. When you are ready, you can begin with the following steps:

Step One: Relax into a comfortable position. Take a few deep breaths and clear your mind of all thoughts.

Step Two: Hold one or two of your hands over the area in your chest just below the collar bone. This is the center of your body's energy vortex and will help you feel more connected to the energy around you.

Step Three: Begin meditating on "seeing" or "hearing" your ancestor, just as you would do when doing other spiritual work. You should begin to notice different kinds of subtle energy in the atmosphere. It is important that you take your time and don't force anything.

Step Four: If your ancestor is present, you may feel it immediately. You can ask them to speak, and he or they may answer you with their own voice or project feelings, thoughts, and images.

Step Five: It is normal for them to try and send extrasensory messages to draw you closer as you work together. They will shower you with love and light, but it is important that you set clear boundaries between yourself and the spirit guides with whom you are working.

Step Six: When you feel the session is finished, it is time to let your ancestor go. You can do this by thanking them for their help, then asking them to leave. You can also do this by using a prayer or other words that you find helpful.

Step Seven: As you finish, close your session with a few minutes of silence and meditation.

The Ascended Masters

The ascended masters are living and very active in the spiritual planes, but they may not be as available to you as a traditional spirit guide. Some people seem to have a closer affinity to these masters than others. If you are one of those people, it may be that your body is ready to resonate with these higher vibrations, but each master will still choose who they want to work with.

It is important to remember that the ascended masters are not exactly masters of magic because they are not from this earthly plane. They are spirit guides who choose to move beyond the physical body but still greatly influence this world. Some people call them ascended because they have risen to a higher level of consciousness, but others say that they have transcended from an earthly plane to a higher dimension.

Ascended masters communicate in many ways. Some may speak to you through your mind, others may appear in your dreams, and others may communicate through signs and symbols. Some may appear physically, but this is the rarest and hard-to-get method of communicating with a master. You can also ask questions, and they will answer them telepathically. If you do not hear the voice within your head, it may manifest as an answer to a question you have been pondering in your mind.

To communicate with masters, you may need to have some personal experience working with spirit guides and some training as a psychic medium. If you are not a trained spiritual worker, you may want to listen and allow the master's access to your mind without trying to analyze the communication.

To begin communicating with these masters, you should use a meditative state in which you turn within yourself and reach out beyond the physical world into an astral realm. You may see images in your mind or hear symbols with which you are not familiar. As you travel within yourself, you may find other types of spirit guides that help to translate messages for the ascended masters.

There are different ways in which these guides can communicate with you, and, in the end, it is up to the master to decide how he or she will engage with you. Once you have identified a master guide who resonates with you, it is important to open yourself to them by consciously thinking about them often. Open your mind to the synchronicities in your life that will help you to recognize their presence. A master's frequent visits are often preceded by intuitive feelings, flashes of light, or even strong smells. If a master does visit in physical form, he or she will likely give you a sign that he or she is there. You may feel a discernible pressure on your shoulder blade, experience sudden goosebumps, or see orbs of light appear out of nowhere.

A master's mission is to guide you down the path of light and enlightenment. He or she will help you to align yourself with your Higher Self. The only reason that a master contacts you is because they believe that you have the potential to do great things in the world. Remember that even if no contact is made initially, it does not mean that a master does not feel there is spiritual potential for growth. It is important not to judge the failure of a master to communicate as an indication that they think you are unfit. Many factors are behind why a master chooses one person over another, and it may simply be that they do not feel you would benefit from their help.

A Totem Animal

The role of a spirit animal is to help you connect with your soul's purpose. Your totem is there to guide you on your journey and keep you focused on the path that was chosen for you. It is best if your relationship with an animal begins in childhood but can also happen later in life. Many people believe that spirit animals choose us rather than the other way around. In your childhood, you may not have been aware that a spirit animal could have been trying to communicate with you through dreams and instincts. As you grow up, however, you may begin to hear them in your subconscious, as these guides can send natural signs and omens to help you take the next step on your journey.

To understand how to work with your totem, it is crucial to understand its role within your life. Your spirit animal is there to act as your guide. The animal's presence can help you to understand the meaning behind certain events in your life. It is particularly helpful when you feel confused – or are experiencing mental fogginess. Its presence can also help to clear your mind so that you can concentrate on being present in the moment.

Your totem animal will often help you to access your subconscious mind. When you feel a strong urge to write or think about something, your spirit animal is likely trying to communicate with you. For example, some people feel compelled to write in their journals when they are sitting in traffic or on a bus. These are very common occurrences for those who have spirit animals. If you want to work with an animal guide, you must be aware of these instinctive impulses and follow them up until they yield more information.

Animals can help us learn how to listen and tune into our intuition. They can send us messages that speak directly to our hearts, and there is no doubt that they can be very wise and intuitive friends. As with any animal guide, you should be open to the messages being communicated to you, as it is likely that they will bring guidance and wisdom to your life.

Elemental Spirits

It is easy to forget that we are all part of a vast universe and that even the air we breathe, the water we drink, and the fire we use are alive. The elementals of nature surround us constantly, but most people do not recognize them as beings at all. This can be a problem, as each elemental has a positive purpose to fulfill in your life. Whether your guides are elemental spirits or not, you must learn how to work with Earth energies and elements. Elemental energies are the building blocks of nature and are very powerful, especially when harnessed by a trained practitioner.

Connecting with the elementals is a very different process than working with other types of guides or spirits. They can be easily identified by their energy which is very different from that of your other guides. They are often less organized than spirit guides, so it is best to work with them consciously rather than allowing them to come in and out of your life without your permission. Elemental energies can be unpredictable, so you must learn how to work carefully with them.

There are many ways to identify the elements you may have in your life. One way is to perform divination, such as scrying or dowsing, or to use a pendulum. You can also simply ask the elemental to introduce itself to you by performing a ritual or spell dedicated to the elemental in question.

Elemental spirits communicate in different ways than other spirits do. The most commonly used method of communication is energy dreams. These dreams are very vivid and intense, unlike normal dreams. They are also quite different from lucid dreaming, though some have reported lucid elementals. Some people have also had experiences with elemental personas, which are essentially an element personified into a human form.

Regardless of the method you use to connect with your elementals, you must approach them respectfully and consciously, ensuring that you respect the power they hold in nature and their individual identities and personalities.

Connecting with Your Higher Self

More and more people are learning to connect with their higher selves or the "I" within. This is a term that different religions and spiritual traditions have used to describe the eternal self or soul, the spark of divinity within each of us. There are many ways that you can connect with this part of yourself. The best way is to meditate and clear your mind of all thoughts and anxiety, relaxing into a state of awareness. You can speak directly to your higher self while in this state. You can also use guided meditation, guided imagery, or hypnosis to connect with your higher self.

Once you have established a connection, you must respect and listen to the messages they give you. These messages are often universal truths that help us understand our purpose, goals, and plans for the future. Sometimes they can be difficult to understand, and you may need a spirit guide to help you interpret the message's meaning. Always remember that your higher self is there to help you, protect you, and show you the way. It is your divine source of light, wisdom, love, and power. This energy often works at the highest levels of Creation and helps guide those who are lost along their spiritual path.

It is also important to remember that your higher self exists in a different dimension. Therefore, it cannot be accessed within the physical body. This can be confusing for some people, who may wonder how their higher self communicates with them if it cannot reside within the body. The key is that the communication does not take place on a physical level and therefore cannot be accessed by physical means.

When you first connect with your spirit guides, you may be surprised by the intensity of their energy. This can be overwhelming if you are not already sensitive to this kind of energy. The best way to deal with the energy is to be open and patient. You can also set yourself up for success by respecting all the different kinds of energy that are present and ensuring that you have time and energy to perform the work of connecting and communicating with them.

Some people find that they begin to consciously work with spirit guides right away, while others need to be more open and sensitive to the idea before communicating with guides. It is crucial that you take your time and find what works best for you because it is unlikely that a guide will force themselves on you if you are not ready for them. You can prepare yourself for the work that is to come by meditating with intention, learning how to commune with spirits, and preparing your home for communication and manifestation.

Conclusion

This book has guided what holy books say is true and the evidence supporting these beliefs. It is a great place to start if you are interested in angels and want an understanding of your faith. I hope this will be an opening for anyone looking for guidance, comfort, or just curious about these beings that are said to have watched over us since the beginning of time.

Reaching out to archangels to work with them does not have to be rocket science, nor does it have to be the domain of only the "holy men and women" who have meditated for years, worn the cloth, or know religious texts from cover to cover. It is something you can do as long as you make sure that you are clear in your intentions – *and believe.*

Belief is a very important factor here, and it is the main thing that many scientific studies and minds are missing when they try to look into the phenomenon of archangels and other spiritual and energy beings around us. If you really want to have a transformative experience, you have to be willing to suspend your disbelief. It may be helpful to keep this endeavor to yourself so that no one makes you feel silly for choosing to reach out to a higher power to make your life easier.

Countless others are doing exactly this, and it is why their lives seem touched with otherworldly grace. There is no reason on this little blue dot that you should not have access to the power and might of archangels. So, choose today to take all that you have learned and put in the work. Odds are, your life will never remain the same once you start, and it will change for the better.

Here's another book by Silvia Hill that you might like

Free Bonus from Silvia Hill available for limited time

Hi Spirituality Lovers!

My name is Silvia Hill, and first off, I want to THANK YOU for reading my book.

Now you have a chance to join my exclusive spirituality email list so you can get the ebooks below for free as well as the potential to get more spirituality ebooks for free! Simply click the link below to join.

P.S. Remember that it's 100% free to join the list.

~~$27~~ FREE BONUSES

💜 9 Types of Spirit Guides and How to Connect to Them

💜 How to Develop Your Intuition: 7 Secrets for Psychic Development and Tarot Reading

💜 Tarot Reading Secrets for Love, Career, and General Messages

Access your free bonuses here
https://livetolearn.lpages.co/archangels-paperback/

References

Berner, C. (2007). The Four (or Seven) Archangels in the First Book of Enoch and Early Jewish Writings of the Second Temple Period. Deuterocanonical and Cognate Literature Yearbook, 2007.

Cline, R. H. (2011). Archangels, Magical Amulets, and the Defense of Late Antique Miletus. Journal of Late Antiquity, 4.

Dix, G. H. (1927). The Seven Archangels and the Seven Spirits: A Study in the Origin, Development, and Messianic Associations of the Two Themes. The Journal of Theological Studies, 28.

Green, M. (2010). The Four Archangels: Angelic Inspiration for a Balanced, Joyous Life. Xlibris Corporation.

Jameson, A. B. (1857). Sacred and Legendary Art: Containing Legends of the Angels and Archangels, the Evangelists, the Apostles, the Doctors of the Church, and St. Mary Magdalene, as Represented in the Fine Arts (Vol. 1). Longmans, Green, and Company.

Łaptaś, M. (2016). Archangel Raphael as protector, demon tamer, guide, and healer. Some aspects of the Archangel's activities in Nubian painting. In Aegyptus et Nubia Christiana. The Włodzimierz Godlewski jubilee volume on the occasion of his 70th birthday (pp. 459-479). Wydawnictwa Uniwersytetu Warszawskiego.

Sandu, I., Iurcovschi, C. T., Sandu, I. G., Vasilache, V., Negru, I. C., Brebu, M., ... & Pelin, V. A. S. I. L. E. (2019). Multianalytical Study for Establishing the Historical Contexts of the Church of the Holy Archangels from Cicau, Alba County, Romania, for its Promotion as a World Heritage Good I. Assessing the preservation-restoration works from the 18th century. Revista de Chimie.

Virtue, D. (2010). Archangels and Ascended Masters. ReadHowYouWant. com.

Virtue, D. (2011). Archangels 101: How to Connect Closely with Archangels Michael, Raphael, Gabriel, Uriel, and Others for Healing, Protection, and Guidance. Hay House Incorporated

Printed in Great Britain
by Amazon

24270999R00066